FLORIDA

Welcome to Florida

Carole Chester

Collins
Glasgow and London

The author and publishers wish to acknowledge the generous assistance
of the director and staff of the Florida Division of Tourism

Cover Photographs

Van Phillips
(top: Florida oranges; upper 1: Cinderella Castle, Disney World;
upper rt: Kennedy Space Center; mid: Sanibel Island; bottom: Corkscrew
Swamp Sanctuary)

Photographs

The J. Allan Cash Photolibrary
pp 39 right, 43 top and bottom right, 81 inset, 91, 118

Florida Division of Tourism
pp 8, 14, 16, 17 left, 31 right, 33 bottom left and right, 39 left, 47 bottom, 58,
61, 62, 70, 90, 94, 95, 102, 113, 114, 119, 121

International Photobank
pp 80–1 background

International Speedway, Daytona
p 69 bottom

Van Phillips
pp 11, 13 right, 17 right, 18, 19, 20, 21, 22, 24, 26, 27, 28, 30, 31 left,
32, 33 top, 43 top and bottom left, 46, 47 top, 52–3, 54–5, 63, 64,
68 bottom, 68–9, 75, 76, 79, 88–9, 96, 101, 106, 111, 112

Picturebank Photo Library Ltd.
pp 12, 13 left, 69 mid

"PICTUREPOINT – LONDON"
p 34

Regional Maps

Mike Shand, Kažia L. Kram, Iain Gerard

Town Plans and Area Maps

M. & R. Piggott

Illustration

pp 6–7 Peter Joyce

ISBN 0 00 447386 8

HOW TO USE THIS BOOK

The contents page of this book shows how the state of Florida is divided up into tourist regions.
The book is in two sections: general information and gazetteer.
In the gazetteer each tourist region has an introduction and
a regional map (detail below left).
There are also plans of the main cities (detail below right) and area
maps of Orlando and the Gold Coast.
The main entries in the gazetteer are shown on the regional maps.
Places to visit and leisure facilities available in each region and city are indicated by symbols.
Main highways, railroads and airports are shown on the maps.

Regional Maps

🖼	Museum/gallery
🏰	Castle/fort
⊞	Interesting building
✝	Religious building
✈ (circled)	Main airport
✈	Other airport
♣	State park
●	Park/recreation area
❖	Gardens
⊛	Theme/amusement park
🐦	Wildlife reserve
🦍	Zoo/safari park

Watersports such as fishing, sailing, canoeing,
etc., are so widespread throughout Florida that
such activities have not been individually
identified.

Town Plans and Area Maps

🖼	Museum/gallery
✝	Religious building
⊞	Interesting building
▣	Theatre
✗	City hall
✉	Post office
i	Information
POL	Police
♠	Park
❖	Garden
●	Station
🚌	Bus depot
⊕	Hospital

═══	four lane divided highway
══	principal highway
──	railroad

Every effort has been made to give you an up-to-date text but changes are constantly occurring
and we will be grateful for any information about changes you may notice on your travels.

CONTENTS

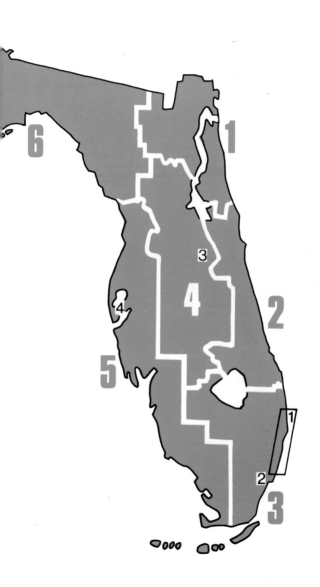

FLORIDA

Whether or not John Cabot (on a charting expedition for the king of England) reached Florida before Juan Ponce de Leon is uncertain, but it is the latter who is generally credited with discovery and the Spanish were certainly the first Europeans to gain the ascendancy there. Already 50 in 1513 when he came upon the peninsula we know as Florida, Ponce de Leon was in search of a legendary 'Fountain of Youth' as well as gold. He and his men first landed somewhere near St. Augustine and worked their way south through the Florida Keys. The Spanish thought that the Florida peninsula was an island – a beautiful one brimming with vegetation and flowers – and they christened it 'La Florida' since it was discovered during the time of the Feast of Flowers. De Leon named the Keys 'The Martyrs' because they looked to him like men suffering.

Neither gold nor the elusive 'Fountain of Youth' was found and ten years elapsed before de Leon mounted another expedition to Florida, this time accompanied by hopeful colonists, cattle and seeds. He landed at Charlotte Harbor, but the embryo colony lasted only five months before it succumbed to illness and attacks by the Indians. (Florida's first Indians were nomadic hunters and fishermen. As their civilization developed, distinct cultures formed in different tribes. The Timucuan culture was the most extensive, spreading throughout the northern part of the state. They and the Apalachee in the northwest established cities, often walled, and raised their own crops. The most ferocious were the Calusa and Mayaimi in the south, who remained nomadic and posed the greatest threat to early European explorers.)

In one particularly violent clash with the Indians, Ponce de Leon himself was wounded and, though the ships set sail for Cuba, he died soon after reaching the island. His epitaph read: In this sepulchre rest the bones of a man who was a lion by name and still more by nature.

Subsequent explorers were even more aggressive in their search for Florida's riches. But their expeditions, too, were ill fated. De Ayllon and his men, for example, were massacred by Indians on their second voyage. De Narvaez was also defeated by Indians when he landed near Tampa in 1528; he lost a third of his force before reaching the site of St. Marks on the Gulf Coast. The rest of his men demanded to go home, but nearly all of them were drowned when their craft was battered by a storm. One survivor, Alvar Nunez Cabeza de Vaca, after wandering for several years

among the Indians in the interior, did eventually manage to return to Spain. He told such marvelous stories of what he had seen, that once again a Spanish expedition set out, this time under Hernando de Soto. He landed in the Tampa region in May of 1539 and his vigorous force took the route north to Ocala and Tallahassee. But the discovery of riches evaded him too and, after 18 months of hardship, he died of fever.

In the spring of 1559 Spain tried again. Several hundred men under the leadership of Don Tristan de Luna reached Pensacola Bay in safety to be wrecked only a few days later. After that failure, the king of Spain decided to desist, at least for the time being.

The next real attempt at colonization was instigated by the French, in 1562, with 150 men under the command of Jean Ribaut. He arrived at Anastasia Island, naming the headland Cap François, then moved to Port Royal Harbor determined to found a settlement. A site was selected and a fort was built but this time starvation put an end to the venture.

Ribaut's second-in-command, de Laudonnière, led the next French venture, in 1564, disembarking at what is today St. Augustine where Fort Caroline was set up. The French were convinced, as the Spaniards before them had been, that Florida's wealth was to be found in the interior and they hurriedly went in search of it without paying enough heed to supplies. When supplies ran out, France at first refused to send help but eventually agreed to send a relieving force under Ribaut with families, seeds and farming tools. But by that time Spain had heard that the French were about to seize Florida and Pedro Menendez was despatched in haste to recapture what the Spanish considered to be their property.

The Spanish contingency arrived first and took Fort Caroline in the face of little resistance. Not content with his easy victory, Menendez went on to butcher everyone at the fort as well as the French relief

fleet. The news of such brutality caused a stir back in Europe. But brutal or not, Menendez proved effective by establishing the first permanent settlement at St. Augustine. He sent out his own exploration parties to open up new posts and by 1567 had enough confidence in his colony to leave for Spain, where he was well rewarded by Philip II for his efforts, but told that he was needed in the Caribbean.

During his year's absence the Florida settlement suffered. The Indians refused to pay a corn tribute demanded by the Spanish and, without corn, the smaller posts dotting the peninsula were unable to survive. Dominic de Gourges, a Huguenot soldier, now took advantage of the colony's decline (and Menendez' absence) and decided to avenge the massacre of Fort Caroline. When Menendez arrived back, in 1568, the garrison no longer existed and de Gourges had fled to the safety of France.

Menendez returned to Spain once more, in 1574, leaving his nephew in charge of the colony, and the Menendez family governed there for 100 years more, but not without trouble from the French, the English and the Indians. Sir Francis Drake, for example, captured St. Augustine in 1586 and the town was captured again, in 1665, by the English Captain John Davies. The Creek Indians of Georgia sided with the English (who by this time had settled in South Carolina) and they made raids deep into Florida as far as the Everglades. Though St. Augustine did not fall to the attacks of 1702 and 1740, towns and missions on the Spanish Trail across northern Florida were destroyed and hundreds of Florida Indians were carried off to be sold as slaves. The Creek invaders, on the other hand, took over the area and became known as Seminoles or 'Runaways'.

In 1762 Cuba fell to the English. Peace was declared in 1763 and, under the terms of the Treaty of Paris, Spain agreed to exchange Florida for Havana. The original Florida Indians were few in number by this time, but the Seminoles, whose ranks had been swelled by runaway slaves, were firmly established and had formed a strong federation. However, thanks to their former alliance with the British and to land grants offered by British financiers, they caused little trouble when British settlers moved in. On the other hand, when Florida was ceded back to Spain at the end of the Revolutionary War, there were numerous clashes between the Spanish and the Indians.

Although Americans helped to organize the Republic of Florida, in 1812, they really wanted the territory for themselves. In 1814, Andrew Jackson invaded the peninsula and took Pensacola. In 1818, he again invaded, seizing Fort St. Marks on the Gulf. In 1821, Florida was annexed to the United States and, in 1823, Tallahassee was chosen as the site of the new capital.

These moves sparked off pressure between white settlers and the Seminoles who occupied the best land in the interior. Frequent outrage and revenge were inevitable, especially as the US made a number of attempts to move the Indians to land west of the Mississippi. Treaties were made only to be broken, and clashes became so violent they soon turned into wars. Between 1835 and 1842, the Seminole Wars cost the US hundreds of lives and millions of dollars. Under great chiefs such as Osceola, Micanopy, Coacoochee, Aripeka and Alligator, the Seminoles fought hard and well, but were gradually driven back into Florida's swamplands and forests. Many were killed or captured and transported west; others fled to deepest wilderness in the Everglades. In 1855 there was one further outbreak of war after US surveyors were sent to the Everglades. It ended when the Federal Government gave the tribe's chief a generous grant to take the majority of his followers west. Those who refused faded back into the swamp, thought to be a dying race. (Actually, their descendants still thrive. The Seminoles today are one of two formally recognized tribes in Florida – the other is the Miccosukee – and they number about 1500 living on five reservations at Tampa, Immokalee, Hollywood, Brighton and Big Cypress.)

By 1845, Florida knew what it had to offer. A slave-owning state, it boasted cotton and sugar plantations. There were cattle and hogs in the west and the growing of citrus fruit was beginning to be taken seriously. Between 1820 and 1860 the population spread and 40 counties were created. By 1860 cotton was the basis of Florida's economy and most people expected the state to secede from the Union along with its southern neighbors. It did, the third state to join the Confederacy, in 1861, and it became the main supplier of food to the southern army. After the Civil War, there were times of poverty, times of trouble with the black people, and it was not until 1881 that the intensive commercial development of Florida began.

It was in the 1880s that railroad and hotel development were initiated by Henry Flagler and Henry Plant, the far-sighted developers, but it wasn't until after World War I that real estate came into its own in this part of the world. Reports of booming profits in real estate brought speculators by the thousand to Florida in high hopes. Between 1920 and 1925 the population increased four times as fast as in any other state. Cheap land turned expensive overnight; paupers became millionaires. The bubble burst in 1926 when the Depression struck.

But recovery came in the 1930s. Paper mills were introduced and refrigeration plants were installed to make possible the widespread marketing of the fruit and vegetables which grew so favorably in this state. Farming turned co-operative and the citrus industry, which had greatly expanded, became regulated by law. Building was resumed and Florida became a noted tourist destination.

It never looked back. The Sunshine State has much to offer today's visitor: beautiful beaches, resorts, parks, gardens and not least the weather; strings of islands and the natural peace of forest, lake and wildlife sanctuary; a host of adventurous sports and activities, a pulsing nightlife and the man-made brilliance of theme parks like Disney World's Magic Kingdom and EPCOT Center.

Seminole Indians

PASSPORTS AND PAPERWORK

UK citizens require a valid 10-year passport (not the one-year Visitor's Card). The British Collective Young Peoples Passport is acceptable for certain groups provided that one person in the group, over the age of 16, also holds a Certificate of Identity. Passport application forms are available from any post office or the Passport Office, Clive House, 70–78 Petty France, London SW1; India Buildings, Water St, Liverpool 2; Olympia House, Upper Dock St, Peterborough and 1st floor, Empire House, 2 West Nile St,

Glasgow. The application must be accompanied by two passport-sized photos and first-time applicants must also send their birth certificate.

Canadian citizens are normally exempt from passport and visa requirements. Other foreign visitors to the US must have a valid visa. Applications in the UK may be made at the American Embassy, Visa Branch, 5 Upper Grosvenor St, London W1 (01 499 7010); and the US Consulate at 3 Regent Terrace, Edinburgh 6 (031 556 8315); or the American Consulate General, Queen House, 14 Queen St, Belfast (0232 228239). All applications should be accompanied by a passport-sized photo.

Each traveler, including those named in a group passport, must complete a separate visa form. A parent or guardian may complete a form for a child under 16. NB: an indefinite tourist visa no longer expires when your passport does. You can present a valid indefinite visa in an expired passport for entry into the US (along with the new valid passport), so long as the visa itself has not been canceled.

No inoculations or vaccinations are necessary unless you are arriving from an infected area. You may be asked for evidence that you intend to leave the US, e.g. a return ticket.

It is advisable to take out in advance insurance to cover health and motoring mishaps; this can be arranged through an insurance company or travel agent.

CURRENCY

The monetary unit in the United States is the dollar ($) which is divided into 100 cents (¢). Coins are issued in 1-, 5-, 10- and 25-cent denominations. A 5-cent piece is known as a 'nickel', a 10-cent piece as a 'dime', and a 25-cent piece as a 'quarter'. Occasionally, you may come across a half dollar (50¢) or a 'Susan B. Anthony' dollar in coin form. Exact change is needed for telephones, stamp machines and, often, city transport.

Paper bills are issued in denominations of 1, 5, 10, 20, 50 and 100 dollars; 2, 500 and 1000 dollars are rarely found. It is wise to carry the smaller notes as obtaining large amounts of change can be difficult, especially when paying cab drivers.

There is no restriction as to how much money you may take in or bring out of the US, although amounts of more than $5000 must be registered with US Customs. Money can be changed at any bank with exchange facilities (all the major ones, including those at airports), anywhere you see 'Exchange', and at most of the top hotels.

Money is best carried in the form of dollar traveler's checks issued by one of the better-known banks or specialist companies, as you may experience difficulty in some places in changing sterling checks.

HOW TO GET THERE

By Air
From the UK Both Miami and Tampa are international gateway cities. (NB: Or-

lando has a brand new international airport, but as yet there is no direct scheduled London–Orlando service.) Direct services from the UK to Miami are offered by Arrow Air, British Airways and Pan American. Arrow Airlines and Pan American offer direct London–Tampa services. Both cities are also served by a number of foreign and domestic airlines, and sometimes by charter flight organized by a tour operator.

Fare structures and costs constantly change, but major airlines feature three classes: First, Business and Economy. In some cases a full-fare-paying Economy passenger will be upgraded to Business class provided that it has not already been booked out.

By Sea
There is no direct crossing from Southampton unless as part of a cruise. Many cruises are available out of Miami to the Bahamas and the Caribbean.

By Car
Traveling by car in Florida is almost an essential as visitor attractions are scattered and hotels are not usually within walking distance. As with the rest of the US, however, the highway and freeway facilities are among the world's finest. Roads are wide and well signposted. Expect to pay tolls on some roads and keep an eye on signs as you can easily miss the correct entrance or exit, especially in and around Miami.

Alamo Rent-a-Car is one of the most popular car rental firms in Florida, though other major companies like Avis, Hertz, Dollar and Thrifty also have numerous rental offices throughout the state and at the airports. Bear in mind American car sizes. While driving on the right should pose no problems for the experienced driver, it *can* take time getting used to in a massive Buick if the car at home is the standard family saloon!

Most car rental agencies require the driver to be 21 and in possession of a valid driver's license. They all offer different priced packages, discount rates, etc., but happily, car rental is lower in Florida than anywhere else in the US. Check whether there is a charge, however, if you are leaving the car at a different point from where you picked it up. Drop-off charges can be high. Many firms have UK offices.

Remember that British car insurance is not valid in the US. Some states require only very limited third party cover. The minimum limit can be as low as $20,000 and is never more than $50,000. Before you leave the UK make sure that you have enough third party liability cover and also adequate personal accident insurance. Consult your own insurance company or travel agent.

The cost of fuel is still less in the US than in the UK. On the other hand, you cannot drive as fast on the highways as at home. The usual speed limit is 55mph. The American Automobile Association and the British AA have a reciprocal arrangement covering breakdown and other services. British AA card members should ensure their card is stamped before leaving the UK. RAC members can take advantage of the Cordon Bleu service which covers breakdowns, etc.

By Plane

Shuttle flights between points in Florida, e.g. Miami and the Keys, are reasonable in cost, but bear in mind that planes are small and bookings in high season are heavy. The following domestic airlines, serving both Miami and Tampa, have representation in the UK: American Airlines, Arrow Airlines, Continental Airlines, Delta Air Lines, Eastern Airlines, Northwest Orient Airlines, Pan American World Airways, Republic Airlines, Trans World Airlines and United Airlines.

By Train

If plans call for a great deal of train travel within the US a USA Rail Pass, purchased prior to departure, is advisable. It entitles the holder to unlimited travel for specific durations at discount prices. Thomas Cook is the British agent for Amtrak.

Miami City is linked into the nationwide Amtrak network and services leave from the Amtrak Station on the northern outskirts of the city, at 8303 NW 37th Ave. Tel: 638 7321. For information about Amtrak services while in Miami, call 371 7738. In Tampa, rail departures are from Tampa Station, close to the waterfront and Interstate 275.

By Bus

The two major bus companies are Greyhound and Continental Trailways (both with UK offices). Both feature travel passes offering discount fares and unlimited travel for specified durations if purchased outside the US. Miami and Tampa are served by both these firms. In Miami, for Greyhound information, call 374 7222, and for Trailways, call 373 6561.

Getting Around Miami

From the airport, Metrobus service is provided to downtown, Coral Gables, Miami Beach, etc., for a fixed fare. Route No. 3 goes downtown and to the port. Route No. 20 travels downtown. Route No. 28 goes to Coral Gables. Route No. 34 heads for Collins Avenue and Coral Gables. For Metrobus information call 638 6700. There is also limousine service from airport to town plus a special chauffeur-driven cadillac service at extra cost.

Taxis are plentiful and, except for airport zone trips, work on the meter. It takes about 20 minutes from airport to downtown.

Downtown itself is covered by taxis and mini buses and a Metrorail service, introduced in 1984, whose first stage covers 21 miles of an elevated rapid transit system. On the South line, Metrorail operates from Dadeland South Station to Government Center Station downtown, providing commuter service to Brickell Ave, and Coral Gables, South Miami and Coconut Grove. North line takes passengers to Hialeah quickly and easily. The rapid transit line is connected to Metromover, a people-mover system.

ACCOMMODATIONS

Florida has something to suit everyone in the way of accommodations. Budget motels along the highways offer car travelers clean, comfortable lodging and the better motels also provide eating and recreational facilities. Motels, after all, are an American 'invention' and can't be beaten for value for money. They are also located along many of Florida's beaches and near popular areas such as the Everglades and Disney World.

The big chain names, e.g. Hyatt and Hilton, have properties in the state, too. Some are more luxurious than others (the Fontainebleau Hilton in Miami Beach, say), but their main advantages are their worldwide reservation system and overseas representation. Many feature family plans: Hilton allows children, regardless of age, to share their parents' room for free; Howard Johnson and Ramada set the age limit at 18; Master Hosts at 12. Within the US top chains use a toll-free booking number. All toll-free numbers may be obtained by calling 1 800 555 1212.

A string of plush hotels lines Collins Avenue, Miami Beach's main thoroughfare. Several of them have built up reputations for fine cuisine and topline entertainment. Familiar names include the Americana, Eden Roc, Beau Rivage, Ivanhoe and Doral hotels.

Florida is particularly rich in resort hotels. While in the UK the word 'resort' is used to indicate a holiday destination, in the US it implies a complex with a host of recreational facilities, often emphasizing a particular sport such as tennis or golf, in its own grounds.

Fontainebleau Hilton

The Breakers, Palm Beach

(l. and rt.) Art Deco hotels, Miami Beach

Although there are too many to mention in detail, the following are recommended. In Miami, Key Biscayne Hotel and Villas has quiet luxury; no nightclub, but a tennis center and an 18-hole golf course. Boca Raton Hotel and Club, at the center of Florida's Gold Coast, was originally designed by the architect Addison Mizner; it houses priceless antiques and has its own golf course and beach. Famous Palm Beach resort names are The Breakers, still opulent but less snobbish than it once was, and The Colony, noted for its food and service. Twenty minutes from West Palm Beach, Palm Beach Polo and Country Club in Wellington is an exclusive complex with innumerable sports facilities. The Fort Lauderdale Intercontinental is a health spa as well as a hotel. Saddlebrook and Innisbrook are two of the great golfing resorts on the west coast.

Self-catering is another possibility. Holiday homes are of a very high standard, often built in complexes with their own golf courses, tennis courts, swimming pools, etc. The newer ones are around or not far from Tampa. Fishing camps are an alternative for the sports minded. Lake County alone encompasses over 1000 named lakes and has at least 30 fishing camps with lakeside cottages. Campsites are numerous and well run. Situated in almost every state park, forest and recreation area, most of them have electrical hookups plus other facilities for a pleasant holiday. An abundance of youth hostels caters to the young budget market. Sites include locations near the Ocala National Forest; Camp Wewa near Orlando; New Smyrna; Epicenter near Disney World.

Self-catering takes on a different aspect when it's on a houseboat. Houseboating in the Everglades, where you can drift along and stay at will, is especially recommended. The boats are well designed, with electricity, refrigerator, kitchen, bathroom and, generally, sleeping facilities for up to eight people. Easy to operate, they have been custom-built to suit the back country areas of the park (for up to seven

Waikiki Motel, Miami Beach

days), though they are not allowed to move in the open waters of Florida Bay or the Gulf of Mexico. There are outlets to stock up on food supplies and fishing tackle in Flamingo, the park's main tourist area.

Three other houseboat operations are: Create-A-Cruise Inc., based in Carrabelle in northwest Florida, which offers rentals on the Gulf of Mexico. For information write Box 13682, Tallahassee, FL 32308. Tel: (904) 893 7249. Also in northwest Florida, visitors may rent houseboats from Home Cruiser Boat Rentals in Fort Walton Beach. Information from P.O. Box 4343, Fort Walton Beach, FL 32549. Tel: (904) 244 5094. And in central Florida you can cruise through Kissimmee's 'Chain of Lakes' on fully-equipped houseboats that sleep six. They are offered by Orlando-Kissimmee Boat Rentals at 2005 Southport Rd, Kissimmee, FL 33402. Tel: (305) 348 4489; or their northern office at 333 South Front St, Wormleysburg, Pennsylvania 17043. Tel: (717) 763 7655.

Holiday apartments, like holiday homes, can be rented in almost all the beach resorts, but an alternative to either the hotel or self-catering holiday is beginning to flourish in Florida – bed and breakfast. The state now boasts several country inns and bed and breakfast networks. In Fernandina Beach, there's a choice of houses; in St Augustine, a choice of inns; and in Inverness (north of Tampa), the Crown Hotel has been renovated in the style of an English country house. Four networks worth noting are: Bed and Breakfast of the Palm Beaches, 205 Circle W., Jupiter, FL 33458. Tel: (305) 746 2545. Suncoast Accommodations, 13700 Gulf Blvd, Madeira Beach, FL 33708. Tel: (813) 393 7020. Tropical Isles Bed and Breakfast, P.O. Box 490382,

Biscayne, FL 33139. Tel: (305) 361 2937. The Bed and Breakfast, 1205 Mariposa Ave, No. 233, Miami, FL 33146. Tel: (305) 661 3270.

Mini-cruising in Florida may be the best of both worlds. Due to the ubiquitous waterways and marinas throughout the state, rental possibilities are too numerous to mention in detail, but here are a few examples. Padelford Packet have introduced the mini-cruise liner, *Viking Explorer*, which sails from Miami to Key West to Flamingo on three-day, one-way cruises. Packages include accommodation, meals, sightseeing and free transportation between Miami and Flamingo. Toll-free reservations within Florida may be made by calling 1 800 328 1472.

A custom-made itinerary is possible out of Daytona Beach with one of the newer boat charter operations. Passengers can select three-day to two-week trips on the St. Johns River, Halifax River or Atlantic Ocean. Information from Silver Glen Springs, Rt. 2, Box 3000, Fort McCoy, FL 32637. Tel: (904) 685 2514.

Two-, three- and four-day cruises on the Orange and Caloosahatchee rivers, on a fully-equipped shallow draft boat that sleeps 16, are featured by a company operating out of Fort Myers. Information from Box 434C, Rt. 29, Fort Myers, FL 33905. Tel: (813) 694 3401.

Leisure sailing through the Keys is just as pleasant. You can choose between a captained charter which includes, boat, captain and food, or a bareboat charter which includes boat and food. Information number is 1 800 327 9385. Adventure sailing through Florida's west coast offshore islands is possible in a flotilla organized by Royal Palm Tours, P.O. Box 06079, Fort Myers, FL 33906. Tel: (813) 489 0344.

FOOD AND DRINK

Citrus fruit has to be the first product which springs to mind when one thinks of Florida. Indeed, nearly 100 billion oranges are grown each year in the state which produces about a quarter of the world's orange crop and supplies 95 percent of orange juice concentrate. Florida is also a leader in grapefruit production with 50 percent of the world's crop. The state yields 80 percent of the globe's supply of processed citrus products, raising enough fruit each year, it is said, to give everyone a pound and a half of citrus each!

Orlando was an early citrus center with the first commercial grove planted close by, in 1865, on 100 acres. It was citrus fruit which first made Florida so important agriculturally, but nowadays the state can also be proud of other fruit and vegetable crops: watermelons, tangerines, limes, mangos, sweetcorn, cucumbers, eggplant, escarole, sweet peppers, radishes and snap beans. The area in Florida devoted to such crops would make an acre-wide strip stretching all the way from Seattle, Washington, to Jacksonville, Florida. The single largest producer of the tropical fruit, mango, is based in Homestead. Tomatoes represent a third of the state's considerable vegetable crop, with many major growing areas around the Ruskin region south of Tampa, and south of Hillsborough County on the Gulf.

All this means quality salads and fresh fruit served in restaurants or sold from roadside stands. It means candied fruits are a good buy and exotic marmalades and jams (like guava) are readily available. It is a fact that if all the fruit and vegetables grown annually were loaded on a single train, the train would have to be 2000 miles long!

Although Florida is by no means a major producer of wine, in recent years it has been experimenting with fruit wines. Growers in Pensacola and Tampa make citrus wines which should be available in local supermarkets and large liquor stores. The state, however, does lead the US in sugar cane production. The largest sugar mill in the US, located at Clewiston, produces some 8.7 million tons of raw sugar annually. And if you have a sweet tooth, look out for Florida honey, particularly the rare white tupelo variety.

Back in the days of the Spanish missions, keeping cattle was as important as growing food crops and it was only when the value of citrus products was realized that cattle ranges were pushed further south. Beef, however, always has been, and still is, an American staple of prime quality. Many Florida menus feature steak with lobster, 'surf 'n' turf', a delicious and filling combination.

Surrounded as it is by water and crisscrossed by so many lakes and rivers, it is hardly surprising that seafood is so popular here. The earliest settlers did not lack a rich and ready supply of shellfish. Once quick-freezing processes had been established, the state's seafood industry became commercially viable. Shrimp and oysters are excellent. So are locally caught clams, mullet and snapper. Florida lobster, actually crawfish, can be bought very reasonably.

There is no shortage of international and ethnic cuisines in Florida, but the Spanish influence is probably the strongest, certainly in Miami and Tampa, both of which boast large Cuban communities. On Calle Ocho, the main artery of Cuban Miami downtown, you can buy hot baked Cuban bread, sweet pastries, strong coffee or a hamburger with french fries inside. Spanish restaurants proliferate in Ybor City, the historic Latin section of Tampa, and the Minorcan influence in St. Augustine still features in the menus of several restaurants there. A Cuban dish as popular in St. Augustine as it is in the Keys is *picadillo*: a mixture of ground beef, olives, raisins and onions served with black beans and rice.

Should you see the word 'scamp' on a Gulf Coast menu, it is *not* meant to be scampi. Scamp is a white flaky fish of the grouper family, considered a delicacy because it is so scarce. Florida's stone crabs are scarce, too, but try them, if you can find them, along with green turtle soup or steak.

Miami's large Jewish community (resident and visiting) ensures that kosher food is first class. The culinary contribution of the American Indian, who originally taught the Spanish how to prepare the vegetables they grew, is seen today in cassava pie and corn fritters – though they may be accompanied by rather more cosmopolitan dishes. All kinds of pepper sauces (introduced to the colonists when peppers were first grown in the state) are standard fare.

What started off as an experiment by a couple of wine growers has become quite successful. There are now four Florida wineries bottling fruit wines (orange, tangerine, grapefruit), plus several brands of two grape varieties, Bunch and Muscadine, first cultivated by the early French settlers. By time of publication, there should be at least one additional winery in Ybor City, called The Wines of St. Augustine Inc. It is housed in restored quarters across from Ybor Square and, like three of the other longer established wineries, offers free tours and tastings. The original four wineries are: Florida Heritage Winery & Vineyards, Box 116, Anthony, FL 32617. Tel: (813) 251 5444. Alaqua Vineyards Inc., Rt. 1, Box 97-C4, Freeport, FL 32493. Tel: (904) 835 2644. Fruit Wines of Florida Inc., 513 S. Florida Ave, Tampa, FL 33602. Tel: (813) 223 1222. Midulla Vineyard Winery, Box 15397, Tampa, FL 33684. Tel: (813) 884 0451.

ENJOY YOURSELF

Auto Racing Tops is Speed Weeks in February at Daytona Beach – two weeks of racing that includes the famous Daytona 500. This is followed by motorcycle racing in the first week of March. Late winter drag racing event is the Gatornationals at Gainesville. And Sebring, in central Florida, hosts the 12 hours of Sebring in March, an important stop on the international circuit for sports car drivers. Swamp buggy races are held in Naples in February and October.

Baseball Number one sport in spring when 18 major league teams come to the state for training. Exhibition games are played in Florida during February, March and early April. Miami is the training camp for the Baltimore Orioles.

Boating There are splendid opportunities for boating of all kinds throughout Florida as there are thousands of miles of tidal shoreline and over 30,000 named lakes, streams and rivers. There are so many marinas it would be impossible to mention them all. Greater Miami itself has navigable canals, private and public marinas and all types of boats for rent. Two examples are sailboats from Dinner Key Marina on Bayshore Dr., Coconut Grove; waterski boats from Crandon Park Marina on Rickenbacker Causeway, Key Biscayne.

Boxing Professional boxing, often at championship level, is a regular feature in Miami.

Canoeing Florida's quiet streams are well suited to canoeing. There are 1711 rivers and streams in the state, amounting to 11,000 miles of water. Canoe and supply rental facilities are available in most state parks.

Canoe trail examples: *(Northeast)* Osceola National Forest; 13-mile Bulow Creek (near Daytona Beach); 4-mile Pellicer Creek (near St. Augustine); 26-mile Santa Fe River (near High Springs); 66 miles of St. Marys River (near Jacksonville).

(Central East Coast) Tomoka River's 16 miles (near Ormond Beach); 14-mile Spruce Creek (near New Smyrna Beach); 8-mile Loxahatchee River (near Jupiter).

(Central) Econlockhatchee River's 22 miles (near Orlando); 25-mile Wekiva River (near Orlando).

(West Coast) Alafia River's 13 miles (near Tampa); 13-mile Blackwater/Royal Palm Hammock Creek (in Collier-Seminole State Park); 7-mile Estero River (near Fort Myers); 4-mile Hickey's Creek (near Fort Myers); 5-mile Little Manatee River (near Tampa); 5-mile Upper Manatee River (near Bradenton); 67 miles of Peace River (begins at Fort Meade); 5-mile Pithlachascotee River (in New Port Richey); 84 miles of Withlacoochee River (begins in Withlacoochee State Forest).

(Northwest) Aucilla River's 19 miles (near Tallahassee); 35-mile Blackwater River (near Rock Creek); 50-mile Chipola River (begins in Florida Caverns State Park); 16-mile Coldwater Creek (near

Jay); 22-mile Econfina Creek (near Marianna); 20-mile Holmes Creek (near Vernon); 73 miles of Upper Ochlockonee River (near Tallahassee); 67 miles of Lower Ochlockonee River (near Tallahassee); 27-mile Perdido River (near Pensacola); 27-mile Shoal River (near Mossy Head); 15-mile Sopchoppy River (in Apalachicola National Forest); 167 miles of Suwannee River (near Lake City); 15-mile Sweetwater/Juniper Creeks (near Munson); 14-mile Wacissa River (begins at Wacissa Springs); 4-mile Wakulla River (near Tallahassee); 58-mile Withlacoochee River (near Valdosta); 50-mile Yellow River (near Crestview); 150 miles of National Seashore – Northwest Florida Gulf Islands.

Cycling With so many parks cycling enthusiasts are well served. Bikes can generally be rented from park outlets and also from resort hotels. In the Miami area there are 100 miles of bicycle paths, including those through pretty Coconut Grove and within Crandon Park.

Dog Racing Greyhound tracks are found throughout the state. *(Northeast)* Jacksonville: Bayard Raceways (Oct.–Dec., March–May); Jacksonville Kennel Club (May–Sept.); Orange Park Greyhound Track (Sept.–Oct., Dec.–March). *(Central East Coast)* Daytona Beach Kennel Club (May–Sept.). *(Southeast)* Miami: Biscayne Park and West Flager Dog Track; Miami Beach Kennel Club; Key West Kennel Club; West Palm Beach: Palm Beach Kennel Club; Hollywood Kennel Club. *(Central)* Casselberry: Seminole Park (May–Sept.); Longwood: Sanford-Orlando Kennel Club (Dec.–May). *(West Coast)* Bonita Springs: Bonita-Fort Myers Corp. (Dec.–April); St. Petersburg Kennel Club (Jan.–May); Sarasota Kennel Club (May–Sept.); Tampa: Associated Outdoor Clubs (Sept.–Jan.). *(Northwest)* Ebro: Washington County Kennel Club (May–Sept.); Monticello: Jefferson County Kennel Club (May–Sept.); Pensacola Greyhound Racing (April–Sept.).

Fishing Florida has a worldwide reputation as an angler's paradise. There are over 8400 miles of tidal coastline for saltwater fishing and some 1200 species of fish can be found. More than 150 varieties of freshwater fish abound.

(Northeast) Largemouth bass are the great attraction, especially in the St. Johns, upper Suwannee and St. Marys rivers as well as in the larger lakes around Gainesville. In midwinter and early spring the same locales are good for speckled perch among others. Spring and summer are best for saltwater fishing – perhaps for dolphin and bonito. Charter and party boats are based at Fernandina Beach, Jacksonville Beach, St. Augustine, Marineland and Flagler Beach.

(Central East Coast) 'Gator' trout from six to 12 pounds are a likely catch in the Banana River and the upper reaches of Indian River. Deep water anglers will find sailfish, dolphin, wahoo and mackerel offshore. Charter fleets for trolling and drift fishing operate out of Ormond Beach, Cocoa, Cocoa Beach, Vero Beach, Fort Pierce and Stuart. Freshwater lake fishing is good on several lakes on the St. Johns River: Lake Hell 'n' Blazes, Sawgrass, Washington, Winder and Ponset.

(Southeast) Lake Okeechobee (530 sq. mi.) probably produces more five-pounder largemouth bass than anywhere else in the state. During the fall and winter speckled perch abound here, too. Canal fishing is popular in this region while mangrove snapper, sand perch, etc., are plentiful along the Intracoastal Waterway. Charter craft for half- or full-day trips are available from Jupiter southward through the Keys. The best departure points in the Keys are: Key Largo, Tavernier, Islamorada, Duck Key, Key Colony Beach, Marathon and Key West. Experienced anglers should enjoy hunting a fish exclusive to Florida, the bonefish. Charters on the mainland are available at Miami Beach, North Miami Beach, Hollywood, Fort Lauderdale, Pompano Beach, Boca Raton, Boynton Beach, Palm Beach, West Palm Beach, Riviera Beach and Jupiter. Offshore, the angler's most popular catch is the sailfish.

(Central) A paradise for anglers seeking largemouth bass. The region is dotted with lakes and two of Florida's largest streams, the Peace and Kissimmee rivers, flow almost its entire length. Lunker bass, bream and catfish abound in lakes near Lakeland, Frostproof, Winter Haven, Sebring, Lake Placid and Leesburg. Boat and tackle rental is available at most lakes and rivers.

(West Coast) Fine freshwater fishing is offered in the rivers which empty into the Gulf. Recommended are the Crystal, Homosassa, Hillsborough, Manatee, Braden and Peace. Game fishing for tarpon is excellent from mid-May to August. Bridges and piers are the best spots for hooking trout, snook, etc. Party boat fishing is popular offshore and charters are available at Tarpon Springs, Dunedin, Clearwater, St. Petersburg Beach, Tampa, Bradenton, Sarasota, Venice and Englewood. Tarpon and snook are also abundant further south in the Ten Thousand Islands reached via Marco, Goodland, Everglades City or Chokoloskee.

(Northwest) There are some of the world's finest saltwater and freshwater fishing grounds along the 200 miles of coastal waters. Saltwater catches range from blue and white marlin, sailfish, dolphin, black-fin tuna to barracuda in grounds reached from Pensacola, Fort Walton Beach, Destin, Panama City and Apalachicola, all of which have charter boats for rent. For bass, Lake Jackson, north of Tallahassee, is probably the country's best known but other lakes recommended for bass and bream are Talquin, Miccosukee, the Dead Lakes and Lake Seminole. Speckled trout can be found in the inshore grass flats along the coast.

There is no closed season in Florida for fresh or saltwater fishing. Freshwater anglers, however, need a license which is available to visitors on a 5-day, 14-day or annual basis. Permits may be obtained in local tackle shops, at fishing camps and marinas, or from the licensing department of any county courthouse. Fishing from a pier is often free, though in some cases there may be a nominal charge. Party boat fishing isn't exorbitant.

Football Florida has two national football league teams, the Miami Dolphins and the Tampa Bay Buccaneers. For good seats in season in Miami, go to the Orange Bowl office in advance at Gate 14, 1900 NW 4th St. Tel: 358 2444. In the fall, college football offers some of the best.

Golf Professional golf tournaments are frequent. Major men's annual tournaments include the Doral-Eastern Open (Miami); Bay Hill Classic (Orlando); Honda-Inverrary Classic (Fort Lauderdale); Tournament Players Championship (Ponte Vedra); Tallahassee Open (Tallahassee); Pensacola Open (Pensacola); Disney World Classic (Lake Buena Vista). In winter the ladies also tour Florida in six major LPGA tournaments. There are many championship courses throughout the state for visitors to play.

Hiking Florida boasts a wealth of state parks and forests crisscrossed with hiking and nature trails (see Parks and Forests).

Horseback Riding Many resorts have their own riding stables. Many of the state parks also have riding trails.

Horse Farms A number of thoroughbred horse farms are located in the Ocala region. Visitors wishing to tour them can contact the Ocala/Marion County Chamber of Commerce, P.O. Box 1210, Ocala, Florida. Tel: (904) 629 8051.

Horse Racing In the southeast there are quarter horse tracks in Pompano Park, Pompano Beach; and thoroughbred tracks at Gulfstream Park, Hallandale; Hialeah Park, Hialeah; Calder Race Course, Miami. On the west coast there are thoroughbred horse tracks at OLDSMAR, Tampa Bay Downs, where the season runs Dec.–March.

Jai-Alai Best places for watching this fast moving sport (a version of the Basque game of pelota) are: *(Central East Coast)* Volusia Jai-Alai Fronton at Daytona Beach, March-Oct.; Fort Pierce, Jan.–March and June-Sept.; Sports Palace at Melbourne, Oct.–Dec. and Jan.–March. *(Southeast)* at Dania, Miami and West Palm Beach. *(Central)* Florida Jai-Alai in Fern Park, Aug.–Dec.; Ocala Jai-Alai at Orange Lake, Jan.–March and June–Oct. *(West Coast)* at Tampa, Jan.–June.

Motor Racing (see Auto Racing)

Polo *The* places are Palm Beach and Boca Raton, from November to early March. (An inexpensive spectator sport.)

Skating Florida has four public skating rinks: Center Ice, Countryside Mall, Clearwater; Polar Palace, Miami; Miami Beach Youth Center (Suns. only), Miami Beach; Sunrise Ice Skating Center, Sunrise, near Fort Lauderdale.

Skin and Scuba Diving Skin diving is available year round in Florida. Possibilities for underwater exploration are unlimited when you consider the long coastline with many bays and reefs plus all the

inland waterways. The best months for skin diving along the coast are May–Sept., though the Keys are excellent every month. Inland diving is probably best in winter when the water is clearer. Inland water in springs, caves and sinkholes remains at a constant temperature of 70° Rental equipment is readily available.

Soccer The state has two professional teams, the Fort Lauderdale Strikers and the Tampa Bay Rowdies.

Tennis Innumerable tennis facilities are found throughout the state in, and outside, resort complexes and racquet clubs. Top resorts always have instructors on the premises.

ENTERTAINMENT

Americans love to be entertained and that means no large resort hotel worth its salt would be without supper clubs with cabaret, cocktail lounges with live music, nightclubs with lavishly costumed revues. Such resort hotels are scattered throughout the state, particularly in and around popular beach centers.

Miami is well known for attracting popular entertainers during the high (winter) season. These days brand new hotels (6000 new hotel rooms were projected in 1982 for completion in 1985) are competing with the established favorites in offering top entertainment and other facilities. One of the most famous spots for glamorous shows is still La Ronde Room at the Fontainebleau Hilton in Miami Beach. Indeed, most of the major hotels along Collins Avenue in Miami Beach have that luxurious Las Vegas touch, albeit without the casinos. Revues reflecting Florida's early days may show a Latin influence or may just be plain star-spangled. Celebrity appearances are usually by well-known singers and dancers.

Miami has just about everything in the way of entertainment from Spanish flamenco to burlesque, from disco to hushed and intimate clubs. Since thousands of Spanish speaking people live in the Miami area, that influence is particularly marked. One famous Spanish supper club is Flamenco on 79th Street.

The whole of the Gold Coast (that's Miami to West Palm Beach) is good for vibrant nightlife full of 'in' places at any given time (though they go 'out' pretty quickly, too). Surprisingly, it is Fort Lauderdale which is said to have more bars, lounges and clubs for its population than any other area in the US. Its own big revue center is the Sunrise Musical Theater in the small town of Sunrise just west of Fort Lauderdale. The Gold Coast also offers a choice of showboats: several offer dinner or cocktail cruises with music and entertainment thrown in.

Major Florida attractions, such as Disney World and Epcot at Orlando, feature almost continuous entertainment which gives scope to the unusual. For example, at the Six Flags Stars Hall of Fame would-be Hollywood hopefuls can take screen tests for popular TV programs. Twice a year, the top performance is chosen and the winner goes to Hollywood, California, for a real tryout in a 20th Century Fox production. At Cypress Gardens there are waterski shows, and at Circus World a Western Stampede features gun and rope twirling plus Indian pageantry. Similarly, frontier days are re-created at Six Gun Territory near Ocala.

EPCOT Center: Spaceship Earth

These are just some of the family entertainments available in central Florida but theme parks elsewhere (e.g. Busch Gardens, Tampa, and Weeki Wachee on the west coast) all have their own shows and amusements (see Young Florida).

Bars and cocktail lounges run the gamut throughout the state. They may have a nautical air like those at Bahia Mar, Fort Lauderdale, they may have a panoramic view, they may simulate a British pub, or they may be rustic in aspect.

Florida's entertainment scene tends more to fun than culture. In Miami, however, the Players State Theater resident repertory company performs at

Coconut Grove Playhouse. Touring plays and musicals are usually to be seen at The Miami Beach Theater for the Performing Arts. Other year-round events and theater take place at the Gusman Cultural Center and the Dade County Auditorium, both in Miami.

The Miami Philharmonic Orchestra performs with guest soloists and conductors during high season at both the Gusman Cultural Center and the Miami Beach Theater for the Performing Arts. The Miami Beach Symphony Orchestra also uses the latter. Several major opera productions are presented annually by the Greater Miami Opera Association, and the Dade County Auditorium is used by the Miami Ballet Company three times a year.

YOUNG FLORIDA

Florida is a state made for family entertainment. There are so many theme and amusement parks that you might think the whole place was called Disney World! One of the main themes is the aquatic park which ranges from marine complexes offering shows to innumerable wet slides and tumbles. Whenever a 'show' is possible, it happens. The best-known attractions are constantly adding new features while brand new amusements seem to pop up annually. With youngsters in mind, here are some of the state's best.

(Northeast)

Marineland of Florida has lots to offer children of all ages. An oceanfront complex, it features a porpoise stadium, Wonders of the Sea exhibit, an Aquatic Bird Pool, an Electric Eel Pavilion, a theater and a Shell Museum. The nautical theme of its Playport will appeal to children aged five to nine – there is a full-sized pirate play ship, a ball crawl, a punching bag forest and an earthquake room. Open daily 8am–6pm. On State A1A between St. Augustine and Daytona Beach. Tel: (904) 471 1111.

Marineland of Florida

St. Augustine Alligator Farm, in operation since 1893, is Florida's oldest attraction (though there are now many similar farms). Here, there are alligators, crocodiles and other exotic animals plus an alligator wrestling show. Wildlife shows hourly. Open 9am–5.30pm, State A1A South, St Augustine.

(Central East Coast)

Kennedy Space Center is fascinating for everyone. You can see the launch areas, a missile and rocket display, spacecraft and lunar vehicles. There are plenty of educational exhibits, free films at the Visitor Center, a restaurant, and 3-D movie theater with a five-story screen. Guided bus tours (2hrs) operate daily. Open 8am until dark. Off US 1, S of Titusville. While in Florida call 800 432 2153 for toll-free launch information.

Kennedy Space Center

(Southeast)

Atlantis, The Water Kingdom is a $16.5 million aquatic park which contains an 11-acre lake at its center. Not surprisingly, watery activities are the main appeal with more than a mile of water slides, water chutes and tube rides. There's an Olympic-sized pool and a wave pool plus two amphitheaters where waterski shows take place. You can try a hot-air balloon ride, try out a kayak or rent another kind of boat, whether pedal, motor or bumper. And there are plenty of electronic games on hand. 2700 Stirling Rd, Hollywood. Tel: (305) 926 1000 for open hours.

Brighton Seminole Indian Reservation, near Lake Okeechobee, lies 16mi. N of Moore Haven. Visitors here can see Florida Indians at work and play, and watch cattle ranching and shows in the special rodeo arena.

Fairchild Tropical Garden is said to be the nation's largest subtropical botanical garden. There are 83 acres of palms, cycads and other exotic plants from around the world. Winding paths take you to the Rain Forest, Vine Pergola, Sunken Garden, Palm Glade and the Rare Plant House, or you can take a guided tram ride through the grounds. Open daily 9.30am–4.30pm. 10901 Old Cutler Rd, Miami. Tel: (305) 667 1651.

Gatorama is an alligator complex with screened walkway through natural habitat. Monkeys and tropical birds are also on display here. S of Palmdale, on US 27.

Hurricane Rapids is a five-story manmade mountain which has three 425-ft concrete flumes winding in and out of six tunnels. At the end of the ride you tumble into a large pool. Homestead, SW of Miami on US 1.

Key West Conch Train Tour is the best way to see picturesque Key West, and it's fun. It highlights all the major points of interest in a 14-mile narrated loop tour, including Audubon's house (the painter lived there in 1832) and Hemingway's house (the writer's home for many years). Tours operate daily 9am–4pm from 501 Front St, Key West. Tel: (305) 294 5161.

Conch train tour, Key West

Lion Country Safari You drive through the compound where some 1000 animals roam free. A children's petting zoo houses baby animals in a separate area and there are aviaries and a reptile park. A variety of rides are available in the park, by boat, train or elephant. Open daily 9.30am–4.30pm. W of West Palm Beach, on US 98. Tel: 793 1084.

Lion Country Safari

Bengal tigers, Metrozoo

Miami Metrozoo is a zoo with no cages, where all the animals live in natural habitats on islands surrounded by moats. Hundreds of animals, including the rare white tigers, birds and reptiles are on display, while for children there's a petting zoo. A monorail system operates round the 25-acre African Plains section allowing visitors a close-up view of Plains' inhabitants. Open daily 10am–5.30pm. 12400 SW 152nd St, Miami. Tel: (305) 251 0401.

Miami Seaquarium is home to 10,000 marine creatures and is one of the best marine parks in the US. It covers 60 landscaped acres beside Biscayne Bay and is both educational and amusing. A three-story glass-windowed tank affords the opportunity to watch training sessions which go to show just how much under-standing can develop between a human and a sea mammal. The Reef Tank also has viewing windows – feeding time is the most interesting. A great variety of sea life is on view in other small wall tanks, and you can catch a Jaws'-eye-view at the Shark Channel.

Sea lions perform faultlessly under the Golden Dome while in the Flipper La-goon dolphins are the much-admired stars. (Dolphins are porpoises, not the fish of the same name.) Shows run almost continuously as they do in the Whale Bowl where, at the time of writing, Lolita the Killer Whale goes through her paces.

At Lost Islands you can see blue herons and pink flamingoes. In the tidepools surrounding the islands barracuda flash by. Snack bars and picnic areas are on the grounds and one admission price covers all displays, shows and monorail ride. Open daily 9am–6.30pm. 4400 Rickenbacker Causeway, Key Biscayne. Tel: (305) 361 5705.

Killer whale, Seaquarium

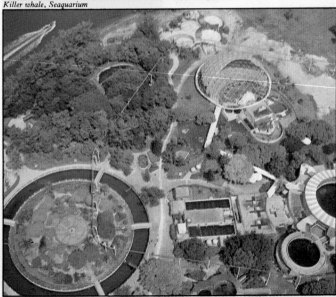

Miami Seaquarium from the air

Miami Serpentarium houses an intriguing collection of reptiles. It has been collecting and processing snake venom for scientific research since 1948. There are daily demonstrations of venom extraction from cobras, rattlesnakes and other poisonous snakes. Open 9am–5pm. 12655 South Dixie Highway, off US 1, Miami. Tel: (305) 235 5722.

Miami Serpentarium

Miccosukee Indian Village There are guided tours of this authentic village of chickee huts (open-sided, thatched huts built on stilts). You can watch Indian crafts being made (and buy if you wish). There are also displays of alligator wrestling. On the Tamiami Trail, 25mi. W of Miami on US 41.

Monkey Jungle

Monkey Jungle lets the monkeys swing free and keeps the people caged. That's right – you walk along caged walkways through an exotic rainforest and it's the tiny wild monkeys who show avid curiosity. You'll also see baboons, gorillas and orang-utans. Chimps are the stars of several daily shows. Open 9.30am–5pm. 14805 SW 216th St, Miami, via US 1 or Florida Turnpike South. Tel: 235 1611.

Museum of Science and Space Planetarium has exhibits of Florida wildlife. Several daily shows are given in the planetarium, and the Southern Cross Observatory telescope atop the building lets you study the stars. Open daily. 3280 South Miami Ave, Miami.

Ocean World is a marine attraction featuring porpoise shows, sea lions, shark tanks and sea life displays. Open daily 10am–4.30pm. SE 17th St Causeway, Fort Lauderdale. Tel: 525 6611.

Orchid Jungle shows a wide variety of species. Jungle trails meander through the huge colorful display. Open daily 8.30am–5.30pm. 26715 SW 157th Ave, Homestead. 25mi. S of Miami, 1mi. off US 1. Tel: (305) 247 4824.

Parrot Jungle

Parrot Jungle is one of Florida's oldest, well-developed attractions. There are over 2000 varieties of plants and flowers growing here and 1000 birds fly about. In the Parrot Bowl there are six daily shows where you can see cockatoos and macaws ride bikes over a high wire, skate and perform a number of other clever tricks. After the show, the pink flamingoes go on parade. Open daily 9.30am–5pm. 11000 South Red Rd (57th Ave), Miami. Tel: (305) 666 7834.

Planet Ocean is maintained by the International Oceanographic Foundation and explains the mysteries of the sea in a particularly novel way with touch-and-explore exhibits, sight and sound shows and push-button games. The producers of the movie, *2001*, have created special film for the audio-visual presentation which uses seven screens and over 23 projectors.

Special effects make Planet Ocean one of Miami's most popular attractions. You can, for example, walk through a hurricane or a rainstorm. No, you don't get blown away or wet through since it's all done with sound and light effects in special tunnels. Similar theme areas offer the experience of entering a drop of water, touching an iceberg or seeing a ghost materialize. Open daily 10am–4.30pm. 3979 Rickenbacker Causeway, Key Biscayne. Tel: (305) 361 9455.

Theater of the Sea is America's second oldest attraction. Marine shows are held in a natural lagoon. Porpoises jump into a 'bottomless' boat. Displays of tidepool creatures and 'encounter' experiences are other features. Islamorada, on US 1, Upper Matecumbe Key.

Vizcaya was once the palatial home of International Harvester magnate, James Deering. Built and decorated in Italian Renaissance style, it contains many fine antiques and paintings. Deering, a bachelor, lived here until his death in 1925. The 70-room Venetian villa is now the Dade County Art Museum, considered by many Americans to be one of the finest of its kind. Set facing Biscayne Bay, it has eight acres of formal gardens with fountains and ornate statuary. Open daily 10am–5pm. 3251 South Miami Ave, Miami. For information on night-time Sound and Light shows (May–Sept.) call 579 2708.

(Central Florida)

(Map of Orlando area, p.100)

Circus World has to be one of central Florida's most enjoyable attractions. Here you will find live circus, circus on screen, traveling circus, fairground shows and thrill rides and participation circus.

Circus World

Clowns meet and greet, perform, parade and help make up the guests in the participation arena. And it's not only the children who leave there with their faces painted! Anyone with the urge to try the high wire or trapeze can do so quite safely in this arena. In another arena elephants perform and offer rides. Circus on screen comes via the huge IMAX seven-story system which gives you that in-the-ring feeling.

Rides range from suitable for tots to the Florida Hurricane, a 3500-ft wooden roller coaster which climbs 95 ft before dipping, when it travels a mile a minute. The Zoomerang is another thrill ride some people could do without: a four-car train catapults from a 50-ft-high platform, makes a full circle loop, climbs another 50 ft and plunges backwards through the loop.

For a change of pace, visit Great Western Stampede and catch a glimpse of the American West – gun twirling, rope and whip tricks, Roman riding and Indian pageantry.

Created by the Ringling Brothers and Barnum and Bailey, Circus World displays unique memorabilia in several historic Ringling railroad cars. Among many restored masterpieces is a 1920s carousel. Open winter 9am–6pm (later in summer). SW of Orlando, at Interstate 4 and US 27. Tel: (305) 422 0643.

Cypress Gardens began in 1936 on a 16-acre tract. Today there are more than 228 acres of botanical gardens and family theme areas. On the botanical side, The Gardens of the World is much favored and in the all-America rose section a number of award-winning varieties grow. Apart from a short period following annual pruning, this display garden is always in bloom, but peak viewing period is between November and Easter.

In the Living Forest, a nature center with live animals and ecology exhibits, you can walk through an aquarium or an aviary, watch an exotic bird revue or alligator show. Kids can ride on pettable animals. Moats and foliage serve as natural barriers between people and animals when necessary while rustic boardwalks give added vantage points.

At Hug Haven, a baby animal nursery, children can ride massive tortoises or cuddle a pygmy horse.

In Southern Crossroads, a simulated antebellum town, 3-D movies are shown in the Garden Cinema. Mystifying illusions are created in a computerized multimedia presentation in Legends of the South where 'ghosts' appear and disappear and animated figures look quite real. It's all done with light refraction, mirrors and trick photography.

Waterski shows are a major feature at Cypress, probably because the man who first created the complex was himself a pioneer in watersports. Ski revues were first held in 1947 and have demanded more and more skill with each passing year. Performances are usually given several times a day. Open 8am–6pm. 3mi. SE of Winter Haven, on State 540. Tel: (813) 324 2111.

DISNEY WORLD

To many people Disney World is 'The Magic Kingdom', made famous in Disneyland, California, but in fact it comprises much more. Recreational areas, hotels, a transportation system and, of course, EPCOT, are additional parts of The World. Efficient management, a staff of thousands and the Disney policy ensure that this vacationland is clean and safe, catering to children and adults of all ages, including those who are handicapped.

Strollers are available for rent in the Stroller Shop on the east side of Main Street at the entrance to the Magic Kingdom, and on the east side of the Entrance Plaza at the France pavilion in EPCOT Center. Wheelchairs are available for rent in the Stroller Shop, Magic Kingdom, and just inside the turnstiles on the left as you enter EPCOT. (Limited availability of strollers and wheelchairs.) Both parks have adequately equipped rest rooms for the disabled.

Lost children are soon found, thanks to an excellent security service. If you lose a child, check with the Baby Care Centers in the Magic Kingdom (next to the Crystal Palace Restaurant on Main St) and EPCOT Center (next to World of Motion in Future World). These baby care centers also have facilities for nursing, changing babies or warming bottles and you can buy such items as you need on the spot: disposable diapers, formula, baby food, etc.

Transportation within Disney World is easy. A monorail system operates between the Transportation and Ticket Center (TTC) and both EPCOT and the Magic Kingdom. From the TTC you can travel direct to the Contemporary Resort and the Polynesian Village (see Accommodations below) by monorail. Buses (free to hotel guests and pass holders) operate from all Disney properties to the TTC and to other areas of Disney World. Buses from the TTC operate until 2am (back to the hotels) and the monorail operates until 10pm and, for the most part, waiting time is minimal. Visitors who stay at properties within the complex benefit most from the transportation system. Although other hotels, such as the newly opened Hyatt, do have some kind of courtesy transport, guests still find themselves having to take taxis.

Accommodations within the complex vary from a full-service hotel to self-catering villas. Closest to the Magic Kingdom (after all, the monorail does run right through the lobby!) is the *Contemporary* with its A-frame structure and atrium lobby. It boasts over 1000 rooms and several restaurants, including a penthouse club featuring particularly slick dinner shows at reasonable prices. It has its own marina, a beach, health club, pools and a fun center plus shops.

The *Polynesian Village*, within easy access of The Kingdom, is as near to Hawaii as you're likely to get in central Florida. Shops and most of the restaurants are located in what they call 'the great ceremonial house' while guest rooms are to be found in flanking 'long houses'. One of the Disney dinner show options, a nightly luau, takes place at Luau Cove here. The Village has its own beach and a marina from where you can take a ferry to the Magic Kingdom. (The monorail also makes a stop here.)

Golfers might well choose the *Golf Resort Hotel*, much smaller and not on the monorail but overlooking the golf courses. Families might prefer the Villas and there are four different types. *Vacation Villas* have one or two bedrooms and feature cathedral-style ceilings. The recreational area is the Villa Center which has a pool, laundry, vending machines and games room; golf carts and/or bikes may be rented. *Club Lake Villas* were really designed for conference delegates, though the one-bedroom suites can sleep five and include a jacuzzi. Guests here use the Lake Buena Vista Club for restaurant and sport facilities. *Fairway Villas*, situated near the Lake Buena Vista golf course, are spacious and probably the most attractive of all the accommodations. *Treehouse Villas* are two-bedroom 'houses on stilts' with an away-from-it-all atmosphere.

The *Fort Wilderness* area of The World doesn't have on-site hotels, but it does have over 800 campsites, most of which are for trailers (campers). There are stores for basic supplies and snack bars in the vicinity, but Disney World itself has no large supermarket.

Another area to stay is *Walt Disney World Village Hotel Plaza* at Lake Buena Vista where several hotels and a shopping complex are located. Because they are within the boundaries of Disney property, guests at any of the following hotels can use the transportation free: the Americana Dutch Resort Hotel, the Viscount, the Royal Plaza, Howard Johnson's Resort Hotel, the Buena Vista Palace, and the Hilton (closest to EPCOT Center). Not far from any of these (but not on Disney property) is the fashionable *Cypress Hyatt Regency*. And on US 192 there are a number of less expensive hotels and motels.

Eating at The World can range from a hotdog bought from a cart to a slap-up

Main Street USA

Showboat

Cinderella Castle in the Magic Kingdom (Background)

meal in a glamorous supper club. The Magic Kingdom and EPCOT have a variety of restaurants (see below), but remember you can't get an alcoholic drink in The Kingdom's eating places (except in the hotels). Outside of these areas, an interesting dining spot is the *Empress Lilly* named for Walt Disney's wife. A replica of a sternwheeler riverboat, the *Empress* has several restaurants: one devoted to seafood, one to meat and the elegant Empress Room.

One of the fun dinner shows is given at Pioneer Hall in Fort Wilderness. Dress is casual and the food strictly American (fried chicken, barbecued ribs, corn on the cob and strawberry shortcake); the revue, family style, encourages singalongs. There is a fixed price for everything except drinks. Similarly, a nightly Polynesian revue, a luau more favored for its entertainers than its food, is held at the Polynesian Village Resort. The Top of the World at the Contemporary always has a slick, professional show. There's a small entertainment charge but you choose your meal from an à la carte menu.

In summer there are always added attractions such as the Main Street Electrical Parade and firework displays. Moonlight cocktail cruises, canoe trips, and a campfire program are other high season features.

Entrance to EPCOT/Magic Kingdom is less complicated than it used to be. Visitors can now buy a one-day ticket for either theme park or a three-day, four-day or five-day World Passport which entitles them to unlimited visits to both parks for the length of time stated on the passport – not necessarily subsequent days. Since the one-day tickets cost $17 (1984 price) for an adult, $16 for a junior (12–17 years), $14 for a child (3–11 years), the three-day passports, $37, $35 and $29 respectively, are a better buy. Those not staying at a Disney-owned resort may have to pay a few dollars more.

Magic Kingdom

The theme park comprises six 'lands'. The first land through the turnstiles is *Main Street USA* where you'll find gift shops, a penny arcade, a cinema showing silent films, and an ice cream parlor. A number of old-fashioned vehicles can be ridden up and down Main Street, including a double-decker bus and horse-drawn trolley. Main Street leads into Town Square, always a hub of activity and a good place for lunch – at the Town Square Cafe, Plaza Restaurant or the Crystal Palace Restaurant which, like the Town Square Cafe, serves full breakfasts as well as other food.

Cinderella Castle is the Magic Kingdom's much photographed landmark. Part of Fantasyland, it houses broadcast facilities, security, etc., and at ground level, King Stefan's sit-down restaurant.

Adventureland boasts some of the most popular rides. Not to be missed, Pirates of the Caribbean takes you on a cruise past all kinds of fantastic audio-animatronic sets. Jungle Cruise is a masterpiece of landscaping and the 'wild animals' seen along the way are most realistic. Tropical Serenade was introduced to Disneyland in 1963 and laid the foundation for subsequent attractions, with its animated birds and Tiki gods. Swiss Family Treehouse must be everyone's idea of the perfect treehouse. The 'tree' was constructed by the props department, but the Spanish moss on its branches is real.

Eating places in Adventureland are all of the fast food and snack variety – tropical juices, sandwiches, etc.

Frontierland re-creates the pioneer days. If you want to see the Diamond Horseshoe Revue (corny but fun), be on the saloon's doorstep first thing. Tickets for the performances (several times daily) are given on a first-come first-served basis, and they're popular. Country Bear Jamboree is a favorite of the very young, and a top Disney attraction. The cast of 20 lifesize audio-animatronic bears put on a really good show. Tom Sawyer Island, in the middle of the Rivers of America, is where the kids can rid themselves of pent-up energy and adults can rest up. Frontierland's big thrill ride is Big Thunder Mountain Railroad, a roller coaster-type ride that won't do a bad back any good, though there are no 360° turns.

The only full-service restaurant in this land is the Diamond Horseshoe before showtimes. Hamburgers and hot dogs are basics at Pecos Bill Cafe; submarine sandwiches and apple pies are on the bill of fare at Aunt Polly's.

Liberty Square separates Frontierland from Fantasyland. Its Hall of Presidents is a particularly lifelike audio-animatronic presentation with great attention to detail. So much so, some people swear that there are actors scattered among the mannequins. A pleasant relief ride on a hot afternoon is on a Liberty Square riverboat down the Rivers of America. But top attraction is the Haunted Mansion where special effects create an excellent, if not scary, ride.

If you want to be waited on for lunch, the colonial-style Liberty Tree Tavern is one of the Kingdom's best places. Fried fish and chicken are staples at the Columbia Harbour House or there's a refreshment stand for sundaes and soft drinks.

Small children will undoubtedly wish to head for *Fantasyland* first. Cinderella's Golden Carrousel is a traditional roundabout, and Dumbo the Flying Elephant and Peter Pan's Flight are aerial journeys strictly for kiddies. Older children seem to prefer the Mad Tea Party where they are whirled around in oversized tea cups. Mr Toad's Wild Ride and Snow White's Adventures are similar inasmuch as you go hurtling through doors and narrowly miss being hit by falling objects. Tiny tots might be scared but, generally speaking, these rides are pure fun.

The two leading attractions, however, are It's a Small World and 20,000 Leagues Under the Sea. The former has delightful dolls representing the children of all nations, colorfully singing and dancing. The latter gives the illusion you are on a submarine.

King Stefan's Banquet Hall in Cinderella Castle is a good place to dine, but you need a reservation. Lunch alternatives are

Future World: Spaceship Earth

World Showcase: Japanese pavilion

fried chicken and fries at the Pinocchio Village Haus or pizza at Lancer's Inn.

An aerial tramway is one way of getting from Fantasyland to *Tomorrowland* where Space Mountain has to be *the* thrill ride. A Disney-version roller coaster that includes special effects – if you can keep your eyes open as the eight-seater 'rocket' goes plummeting from the top of the inside of the dark cone to the bottom. Not advisable for the less-than-healthy, those who get motion sick or those who have just eaten. Children under three are not allowed. A moving pavement exits from Space Mountain past the Home of Future Living.

A trip on the WEDway People-mover takes you alongside or through most of Tomorrowland's major attractions, including Space Mountain where you get a view of the hurtling rockets – before you make up your mind to go on one. Starjets, where you pilot your own spacecraft, is another thrill ride and Mission to Mars is suitable for any age group. Scenes of the tropics are shown at If You Had Wings and the Circle-Vision 360 travel film is particularly worth seeing. Carousel of Progress stars an audio-animatronic family who demonstrate the conveniences of a century of electricity, and the Grand Prix Raceway's 'track' is a safe place for driving.

Fast food and snacks only in this land which includes the Kingdom's largest outlet, Tomorrowland Terrace, where a moonburger may be just the thing. Burgers, dogs and fries are also available at Plaza Pavilion, submarines at the WEDway Space Bar and natural foods at The Lunching Pad.

EPCOT

More geared to adults than the Magic Kingdom. (You can get a drink!) The Center is still expanding: the latest World Showcase country to be represented is Morocco while there is a future site for Spain and, no doubt, others. Living Seas, an addition to Future World, is scheduled to open in 1986. Its 5.7 million gallon tank will re-create a coral reef inhabited by ocean creatures to show how high technology is applied to the undersea world.

As the Magic Kingdom is divided into six themed lands, so EPCOT is divided into Future World and World Showcase. **Future World:** EPCOT's landmark is the giant silvery sphere known as *Spaceship Earth* which dominates the whole park. The 'time' ride inside shows history from 40,000 years ago up to the present, and is worth waiting in line for.

In *Communicore West*, Futurecom shows how information is gathered. Hands-on exhibits demonstrate new technology and visitors can try their hand at the Network Control game or the Chip Cruiser game. In *Communicore East* computers that talk and play games are the focal point of Epcot Computer Central, and in the American Express Travelport touch-sensitive video screens preview holidays round the world. At the Energy Exchange all sources of energy are explored in diverting fashion and in the Future Choice Theater, part of the Electronic Forum, there is instant push-button polling on any given subject by any particular audience.

The Land covers six acres and is concerned with food. Listen to the Land, an unusual but interesting boat ride, demon-

Italian pavilion

German pavilion

strates experimental growing methods and innovative agricultural techniques. Kitchen Kabaret in the same complex is an amusing show with a serious message about nutrition, while another Epcot highlight is the environmental symbiosis film, presented in the Harvest Theater.

Journey into Imagination is a delightful building with a ride showing the arts created by the imagination, and a super 3-D film in which the images are so real that you do feel like reaching out to touch them. At Image Works, in the same complex, the Dreamfinder's School of Drama allows visitors to 'be in pictures' and there is also The Sensor which reacts through light and sound to visitors, and drawing by laser. It is one of the most entertaining sections of EPCOT.

Audio-animatronics is used to relate the story of transportation, past, present and future, in the *World of Motion* and, at the end of the ride, entertaining exhibits show the most important means of 20th-century transportation. In *Horizons* a ride takes visitors into OmniSphere for a voyage through a series of sets depicting various aspects of life in the future. And traveling vehicles pass through the *Universe of Energy* where clever camera techniques create three worthwhile motion pictures.

Future World's only full-service restaurant is The Good Turn whose house specialties are regional American foods. This revolving restaurant gives views of the Listen to the Land boat ride below and serves a complete breakfast besides other meals. The Land pavilion has several snack counters, comprising The Farmers Market, which provide a range of items from stuffed baked potatoes to cheese and fruit platters. Sunrise Terrace Restaurant is the place for fried shrimp and chicken in Communicore West, the Stargate Restaurant for a breakfast pizza in Communicore East. Dividing the two main sections of the park, the Odyssey Restaurant is an upmarket establishment serving mainly American fast food favorites.

World Showcase is a collection of pavilions representing various countries round the world by way of architecture, goods for sale and food; sometimes with entertainment. The *Canada* pavilion features a particularly good Circle-Vision 360 film showing all the country's provinces. Canadian sheepskins are available for purchase at the Northwest Mercantile while Indian artifacts and other souvenirs are on sale at the Trading Post next door.

Eat Canadian and try Le Cellier tucked away on the lowest level of the pavilion, serving among other things tortieres, baked salmon and maple syrup pie. Although it is cafeteria service, this restaurant provides more substantial fare than many of the other fast food outlets. And Labatt's beer is on tap.

The *UK* pavilion incorporates what Americans feel is most British: a pub, a half-timbered high street structure that leans at an angle and a thatched cottage, not to mention several good shops selling fine chinaware, woolen sweaters, British tobaccos and teas. Street entertainers are a key feature, especially the Pearly Band. As one might expect, fish and chips, steak and kidney pie, bangers and mash and sherry trifle are served at the Rose & Crown pub and dining room. Beers and ales include Guinness.

Chinese pavilion

Mexican pavilion

The *French* pavilion includes a replica of the Eiffel Tower and a Paris-style kiosk and pavement cafe. Street entertainment is provided by mimes and an accordionist. A major feature is the five-screen travel film, accompanied by classical French music, in the Palais du Cinema. Plume et Palette, selling art and books, is one of the best World Showcase shops. Perfume and handpainted ties or silk scarves can be bought at La Signature. Epicurean cookware can be found in La Casserole, chocolate at Les Halles and wine, of course, in Le Palais du Vin.

Not surprisingly, France is a popular place to eat. Les Chefs du France is a full-service, first-class restaurant whose menus are supervised by three of the finest French chefs. Nouvelle cuisine is the main style of cooking here. Lunch items include pates and cheeses while dinner suggestions include duck in a wine sauce, salmon mousse in pastry or baked oysters. If this is all too costly, try Au Petit Cafe, in front of the pavilion, ideal for a snack or light meal or the Boulangerie Patisserie for croissants, fruit tarts and chocolate mousse.

Aesthetically, *Japan* has a most pleasing pavilion designed in accordance with traditional symbolic values. The pagoda was modeled after an 8th-century structure in Nara's Horyuji Temple and the torii gate follows the design of the one at the Itsukushima shrine in Hiroshima Bay. Occasionally, Japanese dancers entertain here and the Mitsukoshi Department Store sells just about everything its Japanese parent does. In the Mitsukoshi restaurant complex, one can sample tempura cooking or opt for the teppanyaki dining rooms. On the fast food side, the Yakitori

House is ideal if you like skewered chicken basted in soy sauce, and sake rice wine.

Centerpiece of World Showcase belongs to *America* and simulates a colonial mansion. The sit-down multi-media presentation inside includes super audio-animatronics and is the most technically complex. Folklore from different countries is periodically performed in the lakeside amphitheater in front of the American pavilion, and alongside it Liberty Inn serves staple American fast foods.

A reproduction of the Doge's Palace in Venice forms the *Italy* pavilion which features entertainment in 15-minute shows in which the audience can join. Glassware, leather goods, jewelry and chocolates are the items to buy, but the highlight is a meal in L'Originale Alfredo di Roma where the waiting staff often burst into song and the food is as noteworthy as in the famous restaurant of the same name in Rome. Fettucine all' Alfredo is the specialty, but there are many other choices.

Germany's pavilion brings together features from all over the country, including a glockenspiel and a lively beer hall. A good center for shops, Der Buecherwurm stocks prints, Volkskunst stocks cuckoo clocks and woodcarvings and Der Teddybear has one of the best toy selections. Suessigkeiten provides sweets and biscuits and, naturally, there's a wine shop. Figurines are the major feature at Porzellanhaus and at Glas und Porzellan. The Biergarten in a courtyard setting proves as jolly as any authentic beer hall of an evening. Entertainment comes from musicians in lederhosen and dirndls and there is a wide range of hearty German fare from Westphalian ham, potato dumplings and sauerkraut to all kinds of wursts. On the cheap and quick side, the Bratwurst Stand, alongside the pavilion, sells just that.

China's Circle-Vision 360 film shows fascinating sites in mainland China, including Beijing's Forbidden City, Mongolia, the Great Wall and the Great Buddha of Leshan, plus marvelous photography of Tibet. The presentation is screened in a Disney version of Beijing's Temple of Heaven and the subject matter makes this one of the best of World Showcase attractions.

A large assortment of Chinese merchandise is for sale in an emporium called Bountiful Harvest and Chinese music permeates the whole complex.

A pyramid encloses *Mexico*'s pavilion which is highly atmospheric inside. Designed to simulate a marketplace round a plaza at dusk, there are stands and shops selling a colorful array of Mexican merchandise. Strolling Mariachi bands, inside and out, ensure the music is at the right tempo. Audio-animatronics is at work again in the vignettes which are viewed on the short boat trip within the pyramid where a volcano smolders and thunder and lightning suggest the weather is worse than you think. Overlooking some of the boat-ride effects, the San Angel Inn Restaurant serves tacos, tortillas and also much more sophisticated Mexican cuisine. Quick, cheap tacos are available from the Cantina de San Angel stand outside the pavilion.

Fort Wilderness Primarily the campers' section of Disney World, this woodsy 650-acre site offers a number of sport facilities including large playing fields and volleyball courts. There are riding stables, a marina, canoes for rent, a beach, a jogging trail and a nature trail. Some of these facilities are limited to campers' use, some to guests at Disney-owned hotels, and some are open to all.

A petting farm, entertainment at Pioneer Hall, and two stores stocking necessities and souvenirs are also found here. (The Trading Post's deli counters will make up sandwiches for picnicking.)

River Country Situated at the corner of Bay Lake, this watery recreation area is close to Cypress Point at Fort Wilderness campground. The swimming pool here is the largest in Orange County. Heated in winter, it has two sets of diving rocks plus two high-placed water slides which need guts to use.

Best part of River Country is Bay Cove (Ol' Swimmin' Hole) with rope swings and sundry other devices to send swimmers from an air to a water point. Two flumes, one 260-ft-long and one 160-ft-long, shoot the stalwart into the water quicker than a wink. A flume is an overgrown, steep-sided version of a plain water slide. Control is maintained by sitting up to slow down, lying down to accelerate. A more leisurely trip is White Water Rapids raft ride through a series of chutes and pools in an inner tube.

On the edge of the lake there's a boardwalk nature trail through a cypress swamp, a short white sand beach, and a picnic area. Towels can be rented and there are changing rooms. The main snack stand is Pop's Place. The Waterin' Hole nearby has a more limited selection. Children under 10 years must be accompanied by an adult to River Country, which is a separate attraction with a separate admission charge ($7.25, 1984 price). Or it can be combined with Discovery Island ($9.50).

Discovery Island, on the southeast shore of Bay Lake, is a little oasis (11½ acres) of change of pace from the Kingdom and EPCOT. The main attractions are exotic birds and a host of plants from round the world. It takes about 45 minutes to walk round the island using the boardwalks but it's better to come for longer bringing a picnic meal.

Cranes and cockatoos, swans, pelicans and flamingoes all have their own home sections on the island. At Turtle Beach, a 500-pounder is the largest specimen and at Eagle's Watch the pair of southern bald eagles belongs to a species that nests in the wild only in Florida. Avian Way, a walk-through aviary occupying almost an acre, is the home of the most extensive breeding colony of Scarlet Ibis in the US.

Sport at The World Boating on Bay Lake and the Seven Seas Lagoon is easy with various rental options. Speedboats may be preferable when the weather is very warm. Minimum age is 12 years and you can rent them from the Contemporary Resort, Polynesian Village, Fort Wilderness or Walt Disney World Village marinas. The best sailing conditions are usually found in March and April and the marinas rent out several types of boat. Families will find motorized, canopied pontoon boats best if they are just looking for a pleasant chug. Slow cruises for up to ten people can be made on 16-ft canopy boats, available at the Disney World Village Marina. Ski boats with driver and equipment can be rented at the Fort Wilderness and Contemporary Resort marinas.

Cheapest boat rentals are on pedal boats from all lakeside marinas or trips, for resort guests only, from Fort Wilderness'

Bike Barn along the area's canals. Canoes are rented out by the hour. It takes eight people to paddle an outrigger canoe from the Polynesian Village Marina.

White sand edges parts of the Bay Lake shore at Fort Wilderness, behind the Contemporary Resort, and at the Polynesian Village. All the resort hotels have a swimming pool, sometimes two. Fishing expeditions from Fort Wilderness (two hours) leave twice daily with a maximum capacity of five people per trip. The fee includes gear, driver/guide and refreshments.

Trips on horseback leave hourly from the Fort Wilderness corral and horses are gentle enough for non-riders. Best walking and biking trails are also in this part of the park. Best tennis facilities are at the Contemporary, Golf Resort and Lake Buena Vista Club. Both racquets and balls may be rented and the Contemporary offers instruction in its tennis programs.

The World boasts three fine golf courses: the Magnolia and the Palm, both par 72, flank the Golf Resort Hotel. The Lake Buena Vista course, also par 72, is the shortest and hosts the annual Walt Disney World Classic. For beginners the six-hole Wee Links, a miniature championship course incorporating sand and water traps, trees and greens, was designed for the young. Clubs, balls and shoes may all be rented.

Disney World lies 20 miles SW of Orlando off Interstate 4 and State 192. For general information call (305) 824 4321.

Silver Springs

Florida's Silver Springs has both natural and man-made pleasures. Take a glass-bottom boat ride or a jungle cruise. Visit the Reptile Institute or Deer Park or spend time at the Antique Car Collection. An unusual display is the underwater prehistoric canoes. For water enthusiasts there's Wild Waters: twin flumes, in a figure-eight shape, channel riders along 320 ft of twists and turns into the eye of a 'hurricane'. The football-field-length tunnel is alive with a time, space, light and motion show out of which riders explode into a catch pool. Open daily 9am–dusk. On State 40, 1mi. E of Ocala.

Gatorland Zoo Take a miniature train or walk round the covered bridges and walkways to view alligators and crocodiles. This is actually part of an ever-expanding alligator farming complex. The $50,000 'growing' house, where 1000 'gators spend their second year in a protected environment, became operational in 1983. Designed for viewer appeal, it has large plate glass windows. Open daily, summer 8am–7pm, winter to 6pm. On US 441, between Orlando and Kissimmee. Tel: (305) 855 5496.

Gatorland Zoo

Reptile World Serpentarium features a good number of varieties of snakes and lizards from around the world, displayed outdoors in natural settings. Demonstrations on the handling of vipers and cobras, plus venom extraction, are given several times daily. About 4mi. E of St. Cloud.

Sea World covers more than 125 acres. Focal point is the one-million-gallon seawater performing pool; it can seat 3000 people at the poolside. Whales and dolphins are the star performers here. Other theaters and stadiums feature waterski shows, dancing fountains, seals or even live human entertainment.

In this marine park (claimed to be the world's largest), the World of the Sea and the Pacific Tide Pool are equally fascinat-

Six Gun Territory

Wet 'n' Wild

ing. Exhibits include a 150,000-gallon seawater aquarium which duplicates life on a coral reef; graphics and film explain the sea and its life forms; small tanks provide a close-up look at the more exotic sea life.

Sea World contains a Hawaiian and Japanese village, both authentically re-created. The Hawaiian section is designed round waterfalls and tropical gardens, with outrigger canoes to set the scene and restaurants to suit the mood. The Japanese section has its own tea house, sculpture gardens, costumed Japanese pearl divers and a large shell collection.

Small children will no doubt fall in love with The Deer Park housed in a miniature forest. They can feed the dolphins, sea lions, etc., at special feeder areas. They can whizz to the top of the 400-ft observation tower which rotates. Or they can enjoy Cap'n Kids' World, a water-themed playland that features a 55-ft replica of a Spanish galleon.

Always adding to its exhibits, Sea World recently opened botanical gardens with aviaries displaying rare birds and waterfowl and an alligator pond. Open 9am–10pm in summer, to 7pm the rest of the year. 7007 Sea World Dr., Orlando. Intersection of Interstate 4 and State 528. Tel: (305) 351 0021.

Six Flags Stars Hall of Fame is a large wax museum containing figures of over 200 superstars in more than 100 elaborate sets. Tour Vincent Price's Monster Man-sion and be photographed with the Frankenstein Monster; try the games in the family gallery; or dine on a movie set. Visitors here can take TV screen tests. Video effects and hidden surprises add to the fun for both audience and participants. However, twice a year (under an agreement with 20th Century Fox), a top performance is selected and the winner goes to Hollywood, California, to try out for a role in a real 20th Century Fox production. Open daily 10am–10pm. 6825 Starway Dr., SW of Orlando. Intersection of Interstate 4 and State 528.

Six Gun Territory is a Western-style theme park. Frontier days are re-created with daily gun fights, can-can dancing in the saloon and a host of other shows and rides such as the 164-ft skyride. Open daily. Between Ocala and Silver Springs, on State 40. Tel: (904) 236 2211.

Wet 'n' Wild offers acres of family water fun. You can surf in the Surf Lagoon, take to the bumper cars on water, twist and turn down the 400-ft white water slideway. One of the biggest, fastest slides anywhere is the Kamikaze, a chute over six stories high and as long as a football field. In the Raging Rapids section, adventurers can brave waterfalls, rapids, blustery wind and rain tunnels, wave pools and swirling whirlpools. There is a quieter side to all this at Wet 'n' Wild's beach where paddle, sail and speed boats can be rented. Open daily. 6200 International Dr., Orlando. At Interstate 4 and State 435.

Sunken Gardens, St. Petersburg

(West Coast)

Adventure Island is a seven-acre water theme park with waterfalls, slides, flumes, wave pool plus an arcade and sunbathing area. Open daily in spring and summer, weekends in the fall. 4545 Bougainvillea Ave, Tampa. Tel: (813) 971 7978.

Bellm's Cars and Music of Yesterday shows many items from the Gay 90s and the Roaring 20s: autos, cycles, race cars, dance organs, hurdy gurdies, nickelodeons, and so on. Over 1200 music machines and 170 antique cars from 1897. Open daily 8.30am–6pm (Suns. 9.30am–6pm). 5500 North Tamiami Trail, Sarasota.

Busch Gardens/Dark Continent This 300-acre family entertainment park is a top-rank international zoo and home to 3000 animals. It features seven theme areas with rides, shows and entertainment. The Congo section provides access to the Congo River Rapids Ride via a 320-ft bridge walkway near Claw Island, home to the Bengal tigers. The $6 million water-raft ride carries people down a 'raging river': twelve passenger rafts float free along a 1380-ft course controlled by a sophisticated water system. Open 9.30am–6pm in winter (to 10pm in summer). 3000 Busch Blvd, Tampa. Tel: (813) 971 8282.

Fantasy Isles, next to Fort Myers Shell Factory, features larger-than-life storybook characters. Some 36 characters, including Cinderella and Humpty Dumpty, range in height from 7½ to 40 ft. Some figures are animated, others are part of displays in the 26 outdoor arenas. A steam locomotive replica chugs visitors through the park which also houses puma, otters, alligators and monkeys and presents daily exotic bird shows. On US 41, 4mi. N of Fort Myers. Tel: (813) 997 4202.

Florida's Sunken Gardens exhibit more than 7000 varieties of exotic plants and flowers, including an Orchid House. The gardens also contain an aviary and wildlife collection and the King of Kings wax museum. Open daily 9am–5.30pm. 1825 4th St, North, St. Petersburg. Tel: (813) 896 3186.

Homosassa Springs are natural deep-water springs, with a flow of 70,000 gallons a minute, forming a natural aquarium which is part of a federal fish preserve. You can actually walk underwater amid thousands of fish, cruise along tropical jungle waterways or stroll nature trails. Daily alligator and hippo feedings are of special interest. Open 9.30am–5.30pm. On US 19, Homosassa Springs. Tel: (904) 628 2311.

Jungle Larry's African Safari/Caribbean Gardens A 200-acre botanical park which also houses jungle animals. The gardens are a result of many years planning and cover 50 acres where 200 species of waterfowl and tropical birds roam. Orchids are displayed in Cypress

Bengal tigers in Busch Gardens

Busch Gardens, Tampa

Miracle Strip Amusement Park

Cathedral and in the greenhouse. Four animal sections are: Vanishing Africa, Mighty Amazon Jungle, Tropical Asia and Wonderful Everglades. Open daily 9.30am–5pm. On US 41, Naples. Tel: (813) 262 4053.

Ringling Museum Complex The 68-acre estate of the late circus magnate, John Ringling, who willed it to the state. Now the official State Art Museum of Florida, it includes the Ringlings' own Museum of Art, their palatial home: Ca'd'Zan, the Musuem of the Circus and the Asolo Theater. Open Mon.–Fri. 9am–7pm; Sat. 9am–5pm; Sun. 11am–6pm. On US 41, 3mi. N of downtown Sarasota. Tel: (813) 355 5101.

Tiki Gardens If you fancy a South Seas atmosphere, this is the place, with Land of Pagan Customs and South Sea Island Beauty, a restaurant and gift shops to match the setting. Open daily 9.30am–10.30pm. 196th Ave and Gulf Blvd, Indian Shores. Tel: (813) 595 2567.

Waltzing Waters Tons of water dance to the music in myriad colors inside the Rainbow Palace (outdoors at night). Shows daily from 10am–9pm. Porpoise and waterski shows are also held here. US 41 South San Carlos Park, Fort Myers. Tel: (813) 481 2533.

Weeki Wachee The springs, fifth largest in the state, produce 100,000 gallons of water a minute: There are several theme areas, including The Enchanted Rain Forest, and Weeki Wachee is famous for its underwater 'mermaid' show. There is also a Birds of Prey show, wilderness river cruises and Buccaneer Bay, an aquatic recreation area in operation May–Sept. The Pirate's Revenge here starts in a flume ride from a 40-ft tower. A little too high and fast? Then try rope swinging over the Weeki Wachee River bordered by a 140-ft white sand beach. The under-12s get their own water action rides (on a smaller scale) at Fantasy Island. Open 9am–dusk. US 19 at State 50.

(Northwest)

Miracle Strip Amusement Park has its own Jungleland Zoo and Volcano, wild animals and thrill rides. Top of the Strip is a 203-ft-high observation tower. Open daily spring and summer. W of Panama City, on US 98.

Wakulla Springs has water so clear that you get a perfect view of the marine life from a glass-bottom boat. It is a registered national landmark with an abundance of wildlife. 600,000 gallons flow from underground caverns to form the Wakulla River which was explored by an underwater film crew. Their photographic results are shown to visitors in an enclosed boat as it glides down the river, giving a feeling of floating through underground caverns. Open 9.30am–5.30pm winter (6.30pm summer). 11mi. S of Tallahassee.

SHOPPING

Florida's shops are awash with temptation. Covered complexes protect you from the vagaries of the weather while in the arcades everything the shopper could possibly want is on display. New centers are constantly being built all over the state so you will nowhere be limited in your choice of souvenirs in the boutiques and specialty or gift shops. The number of festivals involving craft markets is so numerous that there is always an opportunity for a bargain or, at least, something different.

One of the popular tourist choices is 163rd Street Shopping Center which spreads over 12 blocks near Collins Avenue in Miami Beach. This air-conditioned mall has plenty of specialty shops and boutiques and includes four major department stores. Bal Harbour is one of the most chic shopping areas in Miami Beach. Its mall is beautifully designed, landscaped with (real) blossoming orange trees, tropical foliage and ferns, and resting places have been provided for the non-shopper. Anyone intent on prestigious purchases can't go far wrong here as there are branches of Saks, Mark Cross and Neiman-Marcus.

South of Bal Harbour, in Surfside, Harding Avenue, two short crammed blocks of elegant stores, is the main shopping district. Another busy Miami Beach shopping street is Arthur Godfrey Road. It is one of the oldest streets in the neighborhood but its galleries and salons are very up to date. The Gold Coast's most famous shopping center is Lincoln Road Mall, Miami Beach, pedestrian only and full of shrubs, it was the earliest of its kind.

Downton Miami's Omni Center, on Biscayne Boulevard, is one of the best of the established centers. You can shop here for French couturier labels, though your money will stretch further at Jordan Marsh or the upmarket branch of J.C. Penney, both large department stores. Sans Souci Plaza, off Biscayne Boulevard, is a sure bet for the fashion conscious.

A famous shopping strip south of Miami is Coral Gables' Miracle Mile where all the leading American brand names in men's and women's clothing are sold. A particularly elegant emporium is Galleria Novita, an eight-story complex between Brickell Avenue and Coral Gables. To reach it, guests at several southeast Florida hotels can take advantage of complimentary limousine service if they want the Beverly Hills style of treatment and the accompanying prices. Shops here sell European designer fashions, one-of-a-kind art works, leather goods, porcelain gifts and offer personalized services.

A visit to Calle Ocho (SW 8th St) may lead you to imagine you're on the island of Cuba. (Buses number 5, 28 and 29 go from downtown Miami to Calle Ocho.) Start at the Douglas entrance to Coral Gables. A host of shops and restaurants are located in this 30-block section of town where the Latin influence is so strong. Bello Plaza, at 25th Avenue, has Spanish-style lamp posts and decorative wooden balconies. Specialty shops and cigar manufacturers surround the Tamiami Shopping Center and Monaco Building between 18th and 19th Avenues. The most popular block is between 16th and 15th Avenues, site of the El Pescador fish market.

Coconut Grove south of Miami is best for boutiques. Head for Commodore Plaza or the highly successful and constantly expanding Mayfair.

Each of the resorts in southern Florida has its own tempting stores and complexes in the towns and in the hotels. One of the most glamorous streets is Las Olas Boulevard, Fort Lauderdale, which extends for about a mile and a half with lots of quality stores. A wide range of merchandise can be found along Sunrise Boulevard in malls such as Sunrise Shopping Center and Sunrise Plaza. Galt Ocean Mile and Plaza is another browsing area. Antiques and resort wear are sold on Lauderdale's seafront and in the Sea Ranch Village Shopping Center.

Top Pompano Beach fashion stores are concentrated in Fashion Square at 23rd Street, or there's Ocean Side Center.

In the heart of Boca Raton, Royal Palm Plaza is built like a Spanish village with a variety of shops lining its tropical walkways.

A charming (and fabled) area for the super-rich is Worth Avenue at the center of elitist Palm Beach. In tune with the resort, the shops are Mediterranean style, strung with bougainvillea.

Shopping arcade, Palm Beach

Gift and souvenir shops are probably at their best in the many theme parks and tourist attractions of central Florida, with Disney World outshining them all. There are many such attractions in this part of Florida and all of them boast at least one gift emporium for 'fun' or impulse buys. Other craft stores are located in the proudly preserved historic quarters of cities like St. Augustine and Pensacola. And, of course, there are souvenir shops along the more newly popular west Florida beaches. One of the more unusual buys is a sponge from Tarpon Springs where a Greek community dives for this bounty from the sea.

THE LANGUAGE

As Americanized as the British may be, not all day-to-day words will be familiar, but it won't take too long to get the general idea that when you want chips, ask for *french fries*, and when you want crisps, ask for *chips*. These days both countries offer salad cream *and* mayonnaise as well as tomato sauce *and* ketchup. Americans know the difference between pancakes and crepes, but if you desire the English (with lemon) variety, stick to *crepes* as American pancakes are thicker and spongier.

If you want a biscuit, ask for a *cookie*. If you ask for a biscuit, you'll get a sort of scone. If you fancy some jelly, request *jello*, for if you ask for jelly you'll be given jam. Happily, eggs and bacon seems to be an international dish, but if you want milk in your coffee, order a *regular*.

Tinned products are always *canned* in the US – that's simple to remember, but translate *zucchini* for courgettes, *eggplant* for aubergine, *rutabaga* for swede. And a *broiled* chop or fish is merely grilled. At the end of it all ask for the *check* (not bill) and pay with a *check* (Americans 'can't spell'), before heading for the *coat check* (not cloakroom), the *washroom* (not cloakroom), and the *rest room* (not toilet). Not necessarily in that order.

Don't worry if you're wearing two *vests*, one is a waistcoat, but a pullover, cardigan and jumper are all *sweaters*. A handbag is both a *purse* and a *pocketbook* and a brooch is a *pin*, but just to confuse you, a purse *is* a purse and a pin *is* a pin. Nobody wears plimsolls, but everyone (regardless of age) wears *sneakers*.

In the area of transport, you'll soon recognize the little variations: *parking lot* for car park, *divided highway* for dual carriageway, *rest area* for lay-by and *railroad* for railway. Mind out for the *trucks* (lorries) and fill up with *gas* (not petrol). Don't park on the *sidewalk* (pavement) to go to the *drugstore* (chemist) and remember to check the *windshield* wipers (instead of windscreen). Al Capone may have been a *hood* but so is your car bonnet, while trunks are put in the *trunk* (not boot).

Should someone ask if you're *in line*, they don't mean are you behaving yourself – just are you queuing. Looking for *cotton* may prove difficult if you seek thread, but okay if you want cotton wool. Don't get lost in the dark or you may need a *flashlight* (not a torch). In some cases Americans have created simpler words – why use the French word 'porter' to carry when someone who hops to the bell (*bellhop*) will do, and *fall* says it all for autumn even if the other seasons stay the same.

Think of a *bus* as a coach as well, rub out with an *eraser*, remember that football is their *soccer* but their football is unique . . . and you've got a head start.

While on the subject of language, it would be appropriate to add here that many Floridian place names are Indian in origin. The words are often descriptive and the following are some you might come across on your travels.

Alachua sinkhole
Alafia hunting river
Apalachicola people on the other side
Apopka potato eating place
Apoxsee tomorrow
Bithio canoe
Caloosahatchee river of the Calusa
Chassahowitzka pumpkin opening place
Chattahoochee marked stones
Chuluota pine island
Econfina natural bridge
Fenholloway high bridge
Hialeah prairie
Hicpochee little prairie
Homosassa place of peppers
Hypoluxo round mound
Iamonia peaceful
Immokalee tumbling water
Istachatta red man
Istokpoga dead man
Lochloosa black dipper
Lokossee bear
Loxahatchee turtle creek
Miami big water
Micanopy head chief
Miomi bitter water
Ocala spring
Ochlockonee yellow water
Ochopee big field
Okahumpka one water
Okaloosa black water
Okeechobee big water
Oklawaha muddy
Opalockee big swamp
Osceola black Indian drink
Pahokee grassy water
Palatka ferry crossing
Panasoffkee deep valley

Pennaway turkey
Seminole runaway
Sopchoppy long twisted stream
Steinhatchee dead man's creek
Tallahassee old town
Telogia palmetto
Thonotosassa place of flints
Thopekaliga fort site
Tsala Apopka trout eating place
Umatilla water rippling over sand
Wacahoota barn
Wausau hunting place
Weekiwachee little spring
Welaka river of lakes
Wetappo broad stream
Wewahitchka water view
Wimco chief water
Withlacoochee little big water
Yalaha orange
Yeehaw wolf

WHAT YOU NEED TO KNOW

Airports Miami International Airport is located on the western outskirts of the city of Miami. The airport has two terminals, the main building and a satellite terminal used for many international flights. Both terminals are linked by travolator, a moving-way for the conveyance of passengers. Hourly express buses link the main terminal with the city center. Tampa International Airport is located off Interstate 275, about a half hour's ride from the city center. Orlando International Airport, handy for Disney World, is situated south of the city. The terminal building has an information service and banking and exchange facilities. Transport into the city from each of the above airports is provided by bus, limousine service or taxi.

Banks Generally open 9am–5pm Mon.–Fri. Closed Sats. Suns. and public holidays (see below). Currency can be exchanged at airports and hotels.

Chambers of Commerce There are more than 200 chambers of commerce in cities throughout Florida. You'll find their addresses and phone numbers in local telephone directories or you can write for a complete list to: the Florida Chamber of Commerce, P.O. Box 5497, Tallahassee, FL 32301. (See also Useful Addresses.) Local chambers can help with on-the-spot information about accommodations, restaurants, shopping, etc. Most also keep lists of language translation resources as an aid to international guests.

Churches Churches of all denominations are found in the large cities. Local newspapers list services and hotels will direct

guests to the nearest church to suit their needs.

Climate Climate ranges from temperate in the north to subtropical in the south. Average January temperatures range from around 52°F in the northwest to 67°F along the lower east coast and 70°F in the Keys. Temperatures in coastal and inland areas can be of a very marked difference, for instance, during the brief cool periods in winter, coastal regions will be warmer than inland areas thanks to the moderating influence of Gulf and Atlantic. Summer climate is temperate and uniform, around 82°F in July in all parts of the state.

Clothing There is little need of formal wear except perhaps at some of the Gold Coast's top resorts, especially in winter. In summer clothes that are cool, casual and comfortable are the best bet. Plenty of sportswear and beachwear are a must, though Florida is a good place to buy resort clothing. For men, a short-sleeved sports shirt and slacks or shorts is the universal choice. A jacket and sweater are useful for the odd chilly spell or to combat the efficiency of the air conditioning.

Credit All major credit cards are accepted at most restaurants, hotels, motels, car rental companies and retail stores throughout Florida.

Drinking The legal drinking age is 19. Bar opening and closing times vary but drinks are available somewhere any time of the day or night.

Electricity The standard supply is 110 volts, 60 cycles AC. Foreigners will need to use an adaptor for shavers, etc.

Emergencies Dial 911. The operator will ask which service you require – police, fire or ambulance.

Gasoline (petrol) is cheaper than in the UK, but sold in US gallons. One US gallon is equivalent to about $\frac{4}{5}$ of an imperial gallon or $3\frac{1}{2}$ litres. Many gas stations close evenings and weekends.

Handicapped Facilities for handicapped people are numerous in the US. They include specially designed hotel rooms, rest rooms (toilets), and easy access to top theme parks and attractions. Write to the chambers of commerce (see above) in the towns where you expect to be staying, they should be able to help with specific useful information in their own areas.

Health The Florida Medical Service provides statewide medical help for visitors day and night throughout the year. Experienced multilingual operators staff a toll-free number (1 800 432 4440) which can be reached from anywhere within the state. Over 300 doctors belong to the scheme and many of them will make hotel calls. In most cases credit cards, insurance and medical tourist cards will be accepted as payment. In view of the possible cost of medical care in the US, travelers are well advised to take out health insurance before leaving home.

Interpreters Multilingual personnel are generally available at international airports, large hotels and department stores but the visitor bureau of any chamber of commerce will help locate one.

Postage Post office hours vary in central city branches and smaller cities or towns. Your hotel will be able to tell you the hours of the closest. If you want mail sent to you in Florida but don't know where you'll be staying in any particular town, have it addressed to your name, c/o General Delivery at the main post office of that town. Such mail must be picked up personally. Stamps may be purchased in hotels, motels, drugstores and terminals as well as at post offices. In some cases, this will be by means of a machine and the correct change must be used.

Public Holidays New Year's Day (1 Jan.), Memorial Day (last Mon. in May), Independence Day (4 July), Labor Day (first Mon. in Sept.), Veterans' Day (11 Nov.), Thanksgiving Day (fourth Thurs. in Nov.), Christmas Day (25 Dec.).

Rest Rooms The standard of cleanliness is very high, as it is elsewhere in the US, in rest rooms (public toilets). There should be no worries about using those in gas stations, diners or in designated areas along the highway.

Shopping Shop hours vary. Suburban malls tend to keep later hours and small stores may well be open on Sundays. Some stores and chain restaurants never close.

Telegrams Most hotels allow domestic telegrams and overseas cablegrams to be sent by phone. Cost of the telephone message will be added to the bill. You can also use the nearest Western Union office.

Telephones Public telephones are located in hotel lobbies, drugstores, restaurants, garages and roadside kiosks. Exact change is needed except in emergencies when caller must dial operator (O). Rates for station-to-station calls (when caller will speak to anyone who answers) are lower than person-to-person calls, when caller wishes to speak to someone specific. A caller can speak to several people in different places simultaneously by requesting a 'conference call' from the operator. In the US, a reverse charge call is known as 'collect'.

Florida has a direct-dial system. Charges are less after 5pm and even lower after 11pm. The overseas operator will tell you when less expensive rates apply.

Time Florida is on Eastern Standard Time (GMT minus 5 hours).

Tipping In restaurants which don't include a service charge, it is customary to tip 15–20 percent of the total. No tips are required in self-service cafeterias. Taxi drivers are tipped 15 percent and porters get 50¢ to $1 per case. Generally, hotels in Florida do not add a service charge to cover gratuities so use your own discretion.

Welcome Centers There are six official Welcome Centers where visitors are given a free sample of Florida juice plus any help they need in planning their itinerary. They are located at: Interstate 95 near Yulee; US 1/US 301 near Hilliard; US 231 near Campbellton; Interstate 75 near Jennings; Interstate 10 near Pensacola; inside the Capitol Building in Tallahassee. Centers are open daily (except Easter, Thanksgiving and Christmas) 8am–5pm.

FESTIVALS AND EVENTS

*The 'cracker' (backwoods pioneer) lived in the days when timber and turpentine were the main state industries, and derived the name from whip cracking, a means of communication which developed into an art.

Northeast
January Gator Bowl Football Classic (Jacksonville). *February* Azalea Festival (Palatka); Battle of Olustee Re-enactment (Olustee); Menendez Day Celebration (St. Augustine). *March* *Cracker Day (Bunnell); Delius Festival (Jacksonville); Gatornationals (Gainesville); River Day (Jacksonville); River Run 15,000 (Jacksonville); Riverside-Avondale Homes Tour (Jacksonville); St. Augustine Jazz Festival (St. Augustine); St. George Street Players' Passion Play (St. Augustine); Tournament Players Championship Golf Tournament (Ponte Vedra Beach). *April* Arts & Crafts Festival (St. Augustine); Beach Festival (Jacksonville Beach); Blessing of the Fleet (St. Augustine); Catfish Festival (Crescent City); District Rodeo (Palatka); Easter Week Festival (St. Augustine); Great Cowford Balloon Race (Jacksonville); Jacksonville Suns (baseball) to August; Murjani Women's Tennis Assn. Championship (Amelia Island); Putnam County Fair (Palatka); River City Arts Festival (Jacksonville); Riverside Art Show, Scottish Highland Games and Gathering of the Clan (Jacksonville); Spring Arts Festival (Gainesville); Women's Tennis Assn. Championship (Ponte Vedra Beach). *May* Evening in St.

Augustine (Thurs–Mons., Memorial Day–Labor Day); Fishing Tournament (St. Augustine) to September; Isle of Eight Flags Shrimp Festival (Fernandina Beach); Jacksonville Firebirds (football) to July; Pioneer Days (High Springs). *June* Cross & Sword State Play (St. Augustine) to August; Mug Race (Palatka to Jacksonville); Northeast Florida Championship Outboard Race (Jacksonville); Spanish Night Watch (St. Augustine); Watermelon Festival (Newberry). *July* 4th July Jacksonville Beach Celebration; Natural Lite Kingfish Tournament (Jacksonville); Shell Show (Jacksonville). *August* Days in Spain (St. Augustine); Opera a la Carte (Jacksonville) to May. *September* Anniversary of the Founding of St. Augustine; Florida Junior College Artist Series (Jacksonville) to May; Jacksonville Symphony, to April; Labor Day Regatta (Jacksonville); Lawnmower Drag Race & Citywide Garage Sale (High Springs); Lipton World of Doubles Tennis Tournament (Ponte Vedra Beach); Mayport and All That Jazz (Jacksonville); Offshore Powerboat Race (St. Augustine); River City Opera (Jacksonville) to April. *October* Civic Music Series (Jacksonville) to April; Columbia County Fair (Lake City); Cracker Day (St. Augustine); Flagler County Fair (Bunnell); Northeast Florida Fair (Callahan); Theater Jacksonville, to May. *November* Alachua County Fair (Gainesville); Fall Arts & Crafts Festival (St. Augustine). *December* Christmas Antiques Show & Sale (Jacksonville); Christmas Grand Illumination Ceremony (St. Augustine); Gator Bowl Festival & Football Classic (Jacksonville); Navy Mayport Open Golf Tournament (Mayport).

Central East Coast

January 24 Hour Pepsi Challenge (Daytona Beach); Astronaut Trail Shell Show (Merritt Island); Heritage Classic & Antique Automobile Show (Daytona Beach); On the Green Art Festival (Fort Pierce); Sandy Shoes Festival (Fort Pierce); South Atlantic Golf Tournament (Ormond Beach). *February* Art Fiesta (New Smyrna Beach); Seafood Festival (Grant); Images Festival of the Arts (New Smyrna Beach); St. Lucie County Fair (Fort Pierce); Speed Weeks/Daytona 500 (Daytona Beach). *March* Bluegrass Festival (Titusville); Canadian Festival (Daytona Beach); Cycle Week (Daytona Beach); De Land Outdoor Art Festival (De Land); Frontier Days (Orange City); Martin County Fair (Stuart); Outdoor Art Festival (Jensen Beach); Speckled Perch Festival (Okeechobee). *April* Cracker Day (De Land); Daytona Beach Music Festi-

val; Easter Beach Run (Daytona Beach); Seaside Art Show (Indialantic); Indian River Festival (Titusville); Jaycee Pro-Am Surfing Festival (Cocoa Beach); Raft Race (Titusville); Space Coast Coin Club Show (Cocoa Beach); Space Congress (Cocoa Beach). *May* Striking Fish Tournament (Daytona Beach); Jetty Park Ocean Regatta (Port Canaveral); Music Festival (Daytona Beach); Sailfish Regatta Week (Stuart); Stuart Sailfish Club's Small Boat Tournament (Stuart). *June* Daytona Beach Municipal Band Concerts; Sea Turtle Watch (Jensen Beach); Summer Music Theater (Daytona Beach); Summer Speed Week (Daytona Beach). *July* Annual Celebration of Apollo 11 launch (Cape Canaveral); Firecracker 400 (Daytona Beach); Firecracker Festival (Melbourne); Florida PGA/General Development Open (Port St. Lucie); 4th July Celebration (Ormond Beach); Paul Revere 250 (Daytona Beach). *September* Boys & Girls Fishing Tournament (Jensen Beach); Cattlemen's Labor Day Rodeo (Okeechobee); Florida Pro International Surfing Contest (Cocoa Beach); Offshore Sportfishing Tournament (Sebastian Inlet); Senior American Fun Festival (Daytona Beach); Shark Fishing Tournament (Port Salerno); Great American Raft Race (Port St. Lucie). *October* Cocoa Village Autumn Art Festival (Cocoa); Daytona Pro-Am (Daytona Beach); Leif Ericsson Day (Jensen Beach); Oktoberfest (Melbourne); Space Coast Coin Club Show (Cocoa Beach). *November* Birthplace of Speed Antique Car Meet (Ormond Beach); European Cucumber Festival (Fort Pierce); Halifax Art Festival (Ormond Beach); IMSA National Championship Finale (Daytona Beach); Riviera Open Golf Tournament (Ormond Beach); Sandpiper Bay Regatta (Port St. Lucie); Space Coast Art Festival (Cocoa Beach). *December* Christmas Boat Parade (De Land); Stuart Sailfish Club Light Tackle Tournament (Stuart); World Karting Winter Enduro Olympics (Daytona Beach).

Southeast

January Annual Rodeo (Homestead); Art Deco Weekend (Miami Beach); Fayre at Vizcaya (Miami); Flagler Day (Fort Lauderdale); Glades Farm Tours (Clewiston); Miami Opera Season; Miracle Mile Art Show (Coral Gables); Orange Bowl Football Classic (Miami); Orange Bowl Football Marathon (Miami); Palm Beach Croquet Club Annual Invitational; Palm Beach Polo & Country Club Season (West Palm Beach); Silver Sailfish Derby of the Palm Beaches (West Palm Beach); Whirlpool LPGA Gold

Carnival time in Miami

Hialeah Park race course

Championship of Deer Creek (Deerfield Beach). *February* Artists Day (Miami); Big Orange Festival (Miami); Arts Festival (Coconut Grove); Doral Eastern Open (Miami); Elizabeth Arden Classic (Miami); Flagler Anniversary Open House (Palm Beach); Insilco Masters of Palm Beach (West Palm Beach); Lynda Carter/Maybelline Tennis Classic (Deerfield Beach); Miami Beach Festival of the Arts; Miami Grand Prix & International Festival of the Americas; Miami International Boat Show; Old Island Days (Key West); Palm Beach Festival (West Palm Beach); South Dade County Fair (Homestead). *March* Art in the Sun Festival (Pompano Beach); Boynton's G.A.L.A. (Boynton Beach); Calle Ocho: Open House Eight (Miami); Carnaval Miami; Chalo 'Nitka Festival & Rodeo (Moore Haven); Dade County Youth Fair, Delray Dunes PGA Pro-Am (Delray Beach); Farm Tours (Homestead); Florida Derby Festival (Hallandale); Hatsume (Delray Beach); Hendry County Fair (Clewiston); International Week (Miami); Inverrary Golf Classic (Lauderhill); Lake Worth Spring Festival; Las Olas Art Festival (Fort Lauderdale); Lignumvitae Blossom Festival (Lignumvitae Key); Orange Blossom Festival (Davie); Palm Beach Festival of the Arts (West Palm Beach); Pioneer Days Antique Car Meet (Lake Worth); Salute to Canada Week (Surfside); Seven Lively Arts Festival (Hollywood); Wheelmen's Winter Rendezvous (Homestead); Winter Harvest (Goulds). *April* Aqualympics (Miami); Black Golf Jubilee (Belle Glade); Cracker Day (Deerfield Beach); Delray Affair (Delray Beach); Week of the Ocean (Fort Lauderdale). *May* Automania (Hollywood); Bounty of the Sea Seafood Festival (Miami); Bromeliad Show & Sale (Coral Gables); Dolphin Scramble (Marathon);

Fishing Rodeo (Pompano Beach); Hall of Fame International Diving Meet (Fort Lauderdale); Key West Arts Alive Show; Metro South Florida Fishing Tournament (Miami); Miami River Regatta; Old Island Roots Celebration (Key West); River Cities Festival (Hialeah); Small Boat Tournament (West Palm Beach); Summer Fishing Contest (West Palm Beach); Summer Fishing Tournament (Pompano Beach). *June* Champion Spark Plug Unlimited Regatta (Key Biscayne); Fern Show & Sale (Coral Gables); Florida State Tennis Championships (Delray Beach); Goombay Festival (Coconut Grove); Hibiscus Show & Sale (Coral Gables); International Bonefish Tournament (Marathon); World's Largest Indoor Flea Market (Miami Beach). *July* Everglades Outdoor Music Festival (Miami), 4th July Celebration (Miami/Miami Beach); Happy Birthday America (Deerfield Beach); Hemingway Days (Key West); Jaycee Shark Tournament (Marathon); Key Biscayne 4th July; Key West Fantasy Swimathon & Freedom Run; Lobster Season (Key West); Miami's Summer Boat Show (Coconut Grove); Old Fashioned Ice Cream Social (Goulds); Pops by the Bay (Miami). *August* Boca Festival Days (Boca Raton); Bon Odori (Delray Beach); Lee Evans Bowling Tournament of the Americas (Miami); Royal Palm Festival (Palm Beach); Trinidad & Tobago Festival (Coconut Grove). *September* Great Coconut Grove Bicycle Race; Oyster Season (Key West); Summer Harbor Festival (Fort Lauderdale). *October* Coconut Grove Banyan Festival; Fiesta Italiana (Miramar); Frangipani Festival (Key West); Hispanic Heritage Festival (Miami); International Water Polo Championships (Fort Lauderdale); Key West Fantasy Fest; Masters Synchronized Swimming Nationals (Fort Lauderdale); Renaissance Fayre (Key Biscayne); Seafood Festival (Marathon); Stone Crab Season (Key West). *November* Field Day & Rodeo (Brighton Seminole Reservation); Broward County Fair (Hollywood); Cornucopia of the Arts at Vizcaya (Coconut Grove); Fall Festival (Goulds); Florida Rodeo USA (Davie); Fort Lauderdale International Boat Show; Harvest (Miami); Sun 'n' Fun Festival; (Hollywood); Jupiter Cup Sailboard Races (Jupiter); Key Colony Beach Sailfish Tournament (Marathon); Miami Greek Festival; South Miami Arts Festival (Miami); St. Sophia Greek Festival (Miami); Winter Fishing Contest (West Palm Beach); Winter Fishing Tournament (Pompano Beach); World's Largest Indoor Flea Market (Miami Beach). *December* Christmas Boat Parade (Boca Raton/Fort Lauderdale/Pompano Beach/ West Palm Beach); Gardening Ramble (Miami); Junior Orange Bowl Festival (Coral Gables); Miccosukee Annual Indian Arts Festival (Miami); Orange Bowl Festival (Miami); Seminole Tribal Fair & Rodeo (Hollywood).

Central Florida

January Scottish Highland Games (Orlando). *February* Arts & Crafts Country Fair (Lake Placid); Art Festival (Mount Dora); Bach Music Festival (Winter Park); Bayhill Golf Classic (Orlando); Black Hills Passion Play (Lake Wales); Central Florida Fair (Orlando); Florida Citrus Festival (Winter Haven); Florida Citrus Squeeze-off (Cypress Gardens); Mardi Gras Festival (Orlando); Orange Cup Regatta (Lakeland); Osceola County Fair & Livestock Show (Kissimmee); Silver Spurs Rodeo (Kissimmee); Southeastern Youth Fair (Ocala); Washington's Birthday Festival (Eustis). *March* Automobile Hall of Fame Week (Sebring); Black Hills Passion Play (Lake Wales); Central Florida Fair (Orlando); County Fair & Flower Show (Eustis); Florida State Championship Bluegrass Festival (Auburndale); Florida Watermelon Assn. 'seed spitting contest' (Cypress Gardens); Fun & Art Festival (Leesburg); Golden Hills Academy International Charity Horse Show (Ocala); Highlands County Fair (Sebring); International Tractor Pull (Ocala); Kissimmee Bluegrass Festival; Pioneer Park Days (Zolpho Springs); Sumter County Fair (Bushnell); Sun 'n' Fun Fly In (Lakeland); 12 Hours of Sebring International Grand Prix of Endurance (Sebring). *April* Antique Auto Show (Mount Dora); Arabian Horse Extravaganza (Ocala); Black Hills Passion Play (Lake Wales); Easter Sunrise Service (Cypress Gardens); Sidewalk Art Show (Lake Wales); Southern Regional Water Ski Tournament (Cypress Gardens). *May* Barefoot Endurance Championships (Cypress Gardens); Boomtown Days (Dunnellon); Classic Car Meet (Cypress Gardens); Florida Delta Glider Championships (Cypress Gardens); Founder's Day (Belleview); Sidewalk Art Festival (Winter Park); Sweetcorn Festival (Zellwood). *June* Kissimmee Boat-a-Cade; River Ranch Acres Rodeo Festival (Lake Wales). *July* God & Country Day (Ocala); Junior All American Water Ski Tournament (Cypress Gardens); Liz Allen Invitational (Groveland); Masters Barefoot Tournament (Cypress Gardens); Silver Spurs Rodeo (Kissimmee). *August* Southern Regional Water Ski Show Tournament (Cypress Gardens); World Delta Glider Championships (Cypress Gardens). *September* Go Kart Grand Prix (Auburndale); Oktoberfest (Orlando). *October* Art Show (Ocala); Autumn Art Festival (Winter Park); Boating Jamboree (Kissimmee); Florida Hotdogging Championships (Cypress Gardens); Ocala Week (Ocala); Osceola Art Festival (Kissimmee); Pioneer Day (Lake Wales); Sidewalk Art Show (Lake Wales); Walesfest (Lake Wales) October or November; Walt Disney World National Team Championship Pro-Am (Lake Buena Vista). *November* Art Festival in the Village (Lake Buena Vista); Arts & Crafts Festival (Longwood); Fall Festival & Christmas Parade (Umatilla); Florida State Air Fair (Kissimmee); Golden Age Games (Sanford); Pioneer Days (Orlando); Sidewalk Art Festival (Sebring). *December* Christmas Candlelight Processional (Lake Buena Vista); Christmas by the Lake (Tavares); Country Art Festival (St. Cloud); Tangerine Bowl Football Classic (Orlando).

West Coast

January All-Florida Fiesta of Arts (Lehigh Acres); Annual Shell Show (Sarasota); Annual Arts & Crafts Show (Cape Coral); Collier County Fishing Tournament (Marco Island); International Kite Flying Contest (Sarasota); Greek Epiphany Day (Tarpon Springs). *February* Annual Outdoor Arts & Crafts Show (Cape Coral); Asolo State Theater Season (Sarasota); Estero Island Shrimp Festival (Fort Myers Beach); Fisherman's Seafood Festival (Everglades City); Florida Strawberry Festival (Plant City); Gasparilla Distance Classic (Tampa); Gasparilla Pirate Invasion (Tampa); Orange Blossom Classic (St. Petersburg); People's Gasparilla (Tampa); St. Petersburg International Folk Fair; Southern Ocean Racing Conference (St. Petersburg); Southland Sweepstakes (St. Petersburg); Swamp Buggy Races (Naples); Winter Equestrian Festival (Tampa); Ybor City Fiesta Day (Tampa). *March* All-Florida Championship Rodeo (Arcadia); Chasco Fiesta (New Port Richey); Fun 'n' Sun (Clearwater); Cracker Festival (Largo); Heather & Thistle Holidays (Dunedin); Festival of States (St. Petersburg); Florida Independent Film & Video Festival (Tampa); Fun 'n' Sun Festival (Clearwater); Gasparilla Sidewalk Art Festival (Tampa); Highland Games (Dunedin); King Neptune's Frolic (Sarasota); Latin America Fiesta (Tampa); Spring Festival (Lehigh); Longboat Key Art Center Show; Mainsail Sidewalk Art Show (St. Petersburg); Medieval Fair (Sarasota); Performing Arts Festival (St. Petersburg); Ponce de Leon Festival (Port Charlotte); Pow Wow Festival (Seminole); Sanibel Island Shell Fair; Spring Orchid Auction & Plant Sale (Sarasota); Tarpon Springs Antique Car Show; Tomato-Snook Festival (Bonita Springs); Tony Lema Golf Tournament Marco Island). *April* Chasco Fiesta Art Festival (New Port Richey); DeSoto Celebration (Bradenton); Island Open Fishing Derby (Sanibel/Captiva Island); Cracker Supper (Largo); Ringling Museums Children's Art Carnival (Sarasota); Tarpon Springs Arts & Crafts Show. *May* Fine Arts Exhibition (Naples); International Sandcastle Contest (Sarasota); Marco Island Boat & Water Festival; New College Music Festival (Sarasota); Quail Run Bluegrass Music Festival (N of Tampa); Peace River Bluegrass Festival (Arcadia); Night of the Full Moon (Sarasota). *June* Bluegrass Jamboree & Arts Festival (Trenton); Celebration of Light (Clearwater); Charlotte Harbor Fishing Tournament (Port Charlotte); Hillsborough Tarpon Tournament (Tampa); Pirate Days (Treasure Island). *July* All-Florida Championship Rodeo (Arcadia); Florida State Championship Bellyflop Contest (Trenton); 4th July Bluegrass Celebration (Tampa); Tampa Bay Bluegrass Festival (Riverview). *August* Fishathon (St. Petersburg). *September* Peace River Bluegrass Music Festival (Arcadia); Pioneer Days (Englewood); Sarasota Sailing Squadron Labor Day Regatta. *October* Country Jubilee (Largo); Florida International Windsurfing Regatta (Port Charlotte); Jazz Holiday (Clearwater); Land O' Lakes Festival (Land O' Lakes); Rattlesnake Festival (San Antonio); Swamp Buggy Races (Naples); Venetian Sun Fiesta (Venice); World's Chicken Pluckin' Championship (Spring Hill); World Parachuting Meet (Zephyrhills).

November Fall Plant Fair (Sarasota); Gulf Beach Arts & Crafts Show (Indian Rocks Beach); International Glendi (Tarpon Springs); Ringling Museum Crafts Festival (Sarasota); Seafood Festival (Madeira Beach). *December* Christmas Boat-A-Cade (Madeira Beach); Florida Tournament of Bands (St. Petersburg); St. Petersburg Boat Show.

Northwest
February Mardi Gras (Pensacola). *April* Cedar Key Art Festival; Flying High Circus (Tallahassee); Old Spanish Trail Festival (Crestview). *May* Festival of the Sea & Sky (Panama City); Fiesta of Five Flags (Pensacola); Florida Folk Festival (White Springs); Gulf Coast Challenge Autocross (Pensacola). *June* Annual Shark Tournament (Destin). *July* Big Bang (Pensacola); Florida State Championship Bellyflop Contest (Trenton); Pensacola International Billfish Tournament. *August* Captain's Billfishing Tournament (Panama City Beach); Fort Walton Beach/Destin Open Billfish Tournament (Fort Walton Beach); Gulf Coast Masters Invitational Billfish Tournament (Pensacola); Pensacola Ladies Billfish Tournament; Fun Day & Possum Festival (Wausau). *September* International Worm Fiddling Contest (Caryville); Labor Day Weekend Show (Trenton); Miracle Strip King Mackerel Tournament (Panama City); Blue Crab Festival (Panacea); 'Spirit of Suwannee' Bluegrass Festival (Live Oak). *October* Western Roundup (Pensacola); Fishing Rodeo, Seafood Festival (Destin); Fall Farm Days (Tallahassee); Northwest Florida Championship Rodeo (Bonifay); Panama City Beach Seafood Festival; Pensacola PGA Open; Seafood Festival (Cedar Key). *November* Blue Angels Air Show (Pensacola); Greek Festival Bazaar (Pensacola); Collard Festival (Ponce de Leon). *December* Snowball Derby (Pensacola).

USEFUL ADDRESSES

(Tel. nos in brackets)

Apopka Area Chamber of Commerce, 180 East Main St, Apopka. (305 886 1441)

Bonita Springs Area Chamber of Commerce, P.O.Box 104, Bonita Springs. (813 992 2943)

Cocoa Beach Area Chamber of Commerce, 431 Riveredge Blvd, Cocoa. (305 636 4262)

Daytona Beach Area Chamber of Commerce, P.O.Box 2775, Daytona Beach. (904 255 0981)

DeSoto County Chamber of Commerce, P.O.Box 149, Arcadia. (813 494 4033)

Disney World, Lake Buena Vista. (305 824 4321)

Everglades Area Chamber of Commerce, P.O.Drawer E, Everglades City. (813 695 3941)

Florida Lower Keys Chamber of Commerce, P.O.Drawer 511, Big Pine Key. (305 872 2411)

Florida Upper Keys Chamber of Commerce, P.O.Box 274-C, Key Largo. (305 451 1414)

Fort Lauderdale/Broward County Chamber of Commerce, P.O.Box 14516, Ft. Lauderdale. (305 462 6000)

Gainesville Area Chamber of Commerce, P.O.Box 1187, Gainesville. (904 372 4305)

Homosassa Springs Area Chamber of Commerce, P.O.Box 1098, Homosassa Springs. (904 628 2666)

Jacksonville Area Chamber of Commerce, P.O.Drawer 329, Jacksonville. (904 396 0100)

Key Biscayne Chamber of Commerce, 95 West McIntire St, Key Biscayne. (305 361 5207)

Key West Discovery, 530 Simonton St, P.O.Box 1452, Key West. (305 294 7713)

Kissimmee-Osceola County Chamber of Commerce, P.O.Box 1982, Kissimmee. (305 847 3174)

Lakeland Area Chamber of Commerce, P.O.Box 3538, Lakeland. (813 688 8551)

Metro-Dade County Tourism Dept., 234 West Flagler St, Miami. (305 579 4694)

Miami Beach Visitor & Convention Authority, 555 17th St, Miami Beach. (305 673 7070)

Greater Miami Hotel & Motel Assn., Dupont Plaza Center, 300 Biscayne Blvd Way, Miami. (305 371 2030)

Okeechobee County Chamber of Commerce, 55 South Parrott Ave, Okeechobee. (813 763 4825)

Orlando Chamber of Commerce, P.O.Box 1234, Orlando. (305 425 1234)

Pensacola Area Chamber of Commerce, P.O.Box 550, Pensacola. (904 438 4081)

Pinellas Suncoast Chamber of Commerce, St. Petersburg-Clearwater Airport. (813 531 4657)

St. Augustine & St. Johns County Chamber of Commerce, 10 Castillo Drive, St. Augustine. (904 829 5681)

St. Petersburg Area Chamber of Commerce, P.O.Box 1371, St. Petersburg. (813 821 4069)

Sanibel-Captiva Islands Chamber of Commerce, P.O.Box 166, Sanibel. (813 472 3232)

Sarasota County Chamber of Commerce, P.O.Box 308, Sarasota. (813 955 8187)

Tallahassee Area Chamber of Commerce, P.O.Box 1639, Tallahassee. (904 224 8116)

Greater Tampa Chamber of Commerce, P.O.Box 420, Tampa. (813 228 7777)

Greater Tampa Convention & Visitors Bureau, 801 East Kennedy Blvd, P.O.Box 420, Tampa. (813 228 7777)

MUSEUMS AND GALLERIES

(Tel. nos in brackets)

(Northeast)

Castillo de San Marcos National Monument explains the history of Spain's impregnable fortress in the New World. Open daily 8am–5.30pm. 1 Castillo Dr., St. Augustine. (904 829 6505). Admission charge.

Cummer Gallery of Art comprises an extensive art collection which includes Meissen porcelain. Open Tues.–Fri. 12–4pm; Sat. 12–5pm; Sun. 2–5pm. 829 Riverside Ave, Jacksonville. (904 356 6857). Free.

Doctor Peck House contains antiques from the period 1565–1763. Open Tues.–Fri. 10am–4pm. 143 St. George St, St. Augustine. (904 829 5064). Admission charge.

Florida State Museum is the south's most prestigious museum of natural history, archeology and ethnography, with an emphasis on man and his environment. Presentation of specimens and objects is in a special gallery. Open Mon.–Sat. 9am–4pm; Sun. 1–5pm. Dept. of University of Florida on Museum Rd, Gainesville. (904 392 1721). Free.

Fort Clinch State Park illustrates the history of the area. Open daily from 9am–5pm. 2601 Atlantic Ave, Fernandina Beach. (904 261 4212). Admission charge.

Fort Matanzas National Monument commemorates the Spanish-French struggle for the area. Open daily 8.30am–5.30pm. State A1A, 14mi. S of St. Augustine. (904 829 5522). Free.

Jacksonville Art Museum features pre-Columbian and African art plus Oriental porcelain. Open Tues., Wed., Fri. 10am–4pm; Thurs. 10am–10pm; weekends 1–5pm. 4160 Boulevard Dr., Jacksonville. (904 398 8336). Free.

Jacksonville Children's Museum also houses a planetarium. Open Tues.–Sat. 9am–5pm; Sun. 1–5pm. 1025 Gulf Life Dr., Jacksonville. (904 996 7061). Free.

Joseph E. Lee Memorial Library-Museum relates the history of black Floridians through displays of manuscripts, documents and photographs. Open

Lightner Museum, St. Augustine

Gardens of Vizcaya Museum, Miami

Flagler Museum, Palm Beach

Edison Museum, Fort Myers

Mon.–Fri. 9am–6pm; Sat. 1–5pm. 1424 E. 17th St, Jacksonville. (904 358 2096). Free.

Kingsley Plantation Historic Site tells the story of plantation life in northeast Florida. Open 7 days a week 9am–5pm. Fort George Island. (904 251 3122). Admission charge.

Lightner Museum is part of the City Hall complex. The key displays are 19th-century decorative arts and a 'Victorian Village'. Open daily. King St, St. Augustine. (904 829 9677). Admission charge.

Oldest House (Tovar House, Webb Bldg Complex) contains a number of historic exhibits including Spanish and English antiques. Open daily 9am–5pm. 271 Charlotte St, St. Augustine. (904 829 5514). Admission charge.

San Augustin Antiguo is a restored Spanish village of the 1700s. Open daily 9am–5.15pm. St. George St, St. Augustine. (904 824 3355). Admission charge.

University Gallery features art from pre-Columbian days to the present. Open Mon.–Fri. 9am–5pm; Sun. 1–5pm. At SW 13th St near 4th Ave, Gainesville, (904 392 0201). Free.

(Central East Coast)

Brevard Museum is a treasure house of Indian and pioneer artifacts in an estate which also features a nature trail. Open Mon.–Fri. 9am–5pm; Sat. 1–4pm. 2201 Michigan Ave, Cocoa. (305 632 1830). Free.

De Land Museum holds large numbers of natural science materials and works of art. Open Mon.–Fri. 1–5pm; Sun. 2–4pm. 449 E. New York Ave, De Land. (904 734 4371). Free.

Florida Institute of Technology Library contains the Medaris collection of World War I memorabilia plus exhibits showing the history of Brevard County. Open Mon.–Thurs. 8–11am; Fri. 8am–5pm; Sat. 9am–5pm; Sun. 2–10pm. On Country Club Rd, Melbourne. (305 723 3701). Free.

Gilbert's Bar House of Refuge/Elliot Museum. The former used to be a life-saving station and has been restored to a museum featuring the area's history. The latter comprises historic shops and vehicles. Both open from 1–5pm. 888 NE MacArthur Blvd, Hutchinson Island, Stuart. (305 287 4256). Admission charge.

Halifax Historical Society Museum features early memorabilia of the area. Open daily 2–5pm. 224 S. Beach St, Daytona Beach. (904 225 6976). Free.

Kennedy Space Center (see p.18).

McLarty Museum concentrates on the cultural history of the area. One of the key exhibits is the gold and silver coins salvaged off the Florida coast. Open Wed. and Sun. 9am–5pm. Located in the Sebastian Inlet State Recreation Area, Wabasso. (305 589 3754). Admission charge.

Museum of Arts and Sciences contains a Cuban art collection in addition to natural science exhibits. Open Mon.–Fri. 9am–5pm; Sat. 12–5pm; Sun. 1–5pm. 1040 Museum Blvd, Daytona Beach. (904 255 0285). Free.

Ormond Beach War Memorial Art Gallery and Gardens displays old quilts, tools and flags. Open daily 2–5pm. 78 E. Granada Ave, Ormond Beach. (904 677 0311). Free.

St. Lucie County Museum contains artifacts from prehistoric to present times. Open Mon.–Fri. 9am–4.30pm; Sun. 1–4pm. 414 Seaway Dr., Fort Pierce. (305 464 6635). Free.

(Southeast)

Audubon House and Gardens commemorate the home of the famous painter and naturalist. Open daily 9am–12pm and 1–5pm. 205 Whitehead St, Key West. (305 294 2116). Admission charge.

Bass Museum of Art houses paintings, tapestries and medieval sculpture. Open Tues.–Sat. 10am–5pm. 2100 Collins Ave, Miami Beach. (305 673 7530). Free.

Broward County Mini-Museum documents the history of the area. Open Mon.–Fri. 9am–5pm. 201 SE 6th St, Fort Lauderdale. (305 765 8572). Free.

Flamingo Gardens/Floyd L. Wray Memorial is an interesting complex which comprises an Everglades museum, transportation museum and features the history of south Florida. Tram rides are available through the botanical gardens. Open daily 9am–5.30pm. 3750 Flamingo Rd, Fort Lauderdale. (305 581 5700). Admission charge.

Fort Lauderdale Historical Society Museum illustrates the history of the area. Open Tues., Thurs., Fri. 10am–

4pm. 850 NE 12th Ave, Fort Lauderdale. (305 463 4431). Free.

Fort Lauderdale Museum of the Arts exhibits Indian artifacts and 19th/20th-century European and American art. Open Tues.–Sat. 10am–4.30pm; Sun. 12–5pm. 426 Las Olas Blvd, Fort Lauderdale. (305 463 5184). Admission charge most days.

Hemingway House and Museum features Hemingway mementoes and memorabilia relating to the history of the Keys. Open daily 9am–5pm. 907 Whitehead St, Key West. (305 296 5811). Admission charge.

Henry Morrison Flagler Museum comprises the white marble mansion and the private railroad car of this famous Floridian who died in 1913. Open Tues.–Sat. 10am–5pm; Sun. 12–5pm. On White-hall Way, Palm Beach. (305 655 2833). Admission charge.

Historical Museum of Southern Florida emphasizes the history of Dade County and southern Florida. Open Mon.–Sat. 9am–5pm; Sun. 12.30–5pm. 3280 S. Miami Ave, Miami. (305 854 4681). Free.

Lawrence E. Will Museum tells the history of the Glades area. Open Mon.–Sat. 1–5pm. 530 S. Main St, Belle Glade. (305 996 3453). Free.

Lighthouse Military Museum contains a host of military artifacts including a two-man submarine. Open daily 9.30am–5pm. 938 Whitehead St, Key West. (305 294 0012). Admission charge.

Lowe Art Gallery exhibits a range of art works from American Indian to Baroque and Renaissance. Open Mon.–Fri. 12–5pm; Sat. 10am–5pm; Sun. 2–5pm. 1301 Miller Dr., Coral Gables. (305 284 3535). Free.

Martello Gallery and Museum has a gallery of local art and museum of local history of the Keys. Open daily 9.30am–5pm. On S. Roosevelt Blvd, Key West. (305 296 3913). Admission charge.

Metropolitan Museum and Art Center specializes in Oriental, African and pre-Columbian art. Open Mon.–Thurs. 10am–9.30pm; weekends 1–6pm. 7867 N. Kendall Dr., Miami. (305 271 8450). Free.

Museum of Science features extensive natural science displays and also has its own planetarium. Open Mon.–Sat. 9am–10pm; Sun. 12.30–10pm. 3280 S. Miami Ave, Miami. (305 854 4242). Museum free (charge for planetarium shows).

Norton Gallery and School of Art offers a variety of paintings from Chinese to American. Open weekends 1–5pm. 1451 S. Olive Ave, West Palm Beach. (305 832 5194). Free.

Old Coffee Mill and Florida Railroad

Museum includes historic mill, drugstore and cigar factory. Open Mon.–Sat. 11am–5pm. 512 Greene St, Key West. (305 294 6769). Admission charge.

Science Museum and Planetarium of Palm Beach County shows local artifacts, minerals and fossils. Open Tues.–Sun. 10am–5pm and Tues.–Thurs. 6.30–10pm. 1141 W. Lakewood Rd, West Palm Beach. (205 832 1988). Admission charge.

Society of the Four Arts frequently changes its art exhibits. Open Mon.–Fri. 10am–5pm; Sun. 2–5pm. At Four Arts Plaza, Palm Beach. (305 655 7226). Free.

Vizcaya Museum of Art and Gardens is a European-style mansion with period furnishings, works of art and 16th-19th-century textiles plus formal gardens. 3251 S. Miami Ave, Miami. (305 854 3531). Admission charge.

(Central Florida)

Art Center at Maitland displays paintings, sculpture and graphics. Open Tues.–Sat. 10am–4pm. 231 W. Packwood Ave, Maitland. (305 645 2181). Free.

Beal-Maltbie Shell Museum is unusual inasmuch as it houses one of the world's biggest shell collections. Open Tues. and Sun. 1–5pm; Wed.–Sat. 10am–5pm. Holt Ave, Rollins College, Winter Park. (305 246 2364). Admission charge.

Dade Battlefield Historic Site portrays the history of the Second Seminole War and the battle of 1835 which destroyed Maj. Francis Dade's command. Open daily 9am–5pm. On US 301 S., Bushnell. (904 793 4781). Admission charge.

Early American Museum features restored vehicles. Open daily 9am–9pm. State 40 E, Silver Springs. (904 236 2404). Admission charge.

John Young Museum and Planetarium is one of Florida's top complexes for all the sciences. Open Mon.–Thurs. 9am–5pm; Fri. 9am–9pm; weekends 12–5pm. 810 E. Rollins St, Orlando. (305 896 7151). Admission charge.

Lake County Historical Society Museum displays antiques and photographs of early Lake County. Open Mon.–Sat. 1–4pm. 325 N. New Hampshire Ave, Tavares. Free.

Museum of Old Dolls and Toys is what it says and exhibits span three centuries. Open Mon.–Sat. 10am–6pm; Sun. 12–5pm. 1530 6th St, NW, Winter Haven. (813 299 1830). Admission charge.

Orange County Historical Museum houses artifacts related to the history of central Florida. Open Mon.–Fri. 10am–5pm. 812 E. Rollins St, Orlando. (305 898 8320). Free.

Pioneer Florida Museum houses exhibits relating to Florida's pioneering days. Open Tues.–Sat. 1–5pm. US 301 N, Dade City. (904 567 0262). Admission charge.

Polk Public Museum exhibits textiles, sculpture and artifacts. Open Tues.–Fri. 10am–5pm; weekends 1.30–5.30pm. 800 E. Palmetto, Lakeland. (813 688 7744).

USA of Yesterday offers extensive machinery and Americana exhibits. Open Mon.–Fri. 9am–5.30pm; Sun. 1–5.30pm. US (Alt.) 27, Dundee. (813 439 1731). Admission charge.

(West Coast)

Bellm's Cars and Music of Yesterday holds almost 200 antique, classic and special cars plus 1300 music machines and other antiques. Open Mon.–Sat. 8.30am–6pm; Sun. 9.30am–6pm. 5500 North Tamiami Trail, Sarasota. (813 355 6228). Admission charge.

DeSoto National Memorial shows Indian artifacts and 16th-century Spanish weaponry. Open 7 days a week 8am–5pm. End of 75th St, NW, Bradenton. (813 792 0458). Free.

Edison Home and Museum is the refurbished home of the well-known inventor. Many of his inventions and personal memorabilia are on display here. Open Mon.–Sat. 9am–4pm; Sun. 12.30–4pm. 2350 McGregor Blvd, Fort Myers. (813 334 3614). Admission charge.

Florida Center for the Arts shows pre-Columbian and 20th-century art. Open Mon.–Fri. 8am–5pm. 4202 E. Fowler Ave, Tampa. (813 974 2375). Free.

Florida Gulf Coast Art Center features a variety of art works. Open Tues.–Sat. 10am–4pm; Sun. 3–5pm. 222 Ponce de Leon, Clearwater. (813 584 8634). Donation expected.

Henry B. Plant Museum exhibits artifacts from the area plus furniture and Wedgwood collections. Open Tues.–Sat. 10am–12pm and 2–4pm. In winter, Sun. 2–4pm. 401 W. Kennedy St, Tampa. (813 253 8861). Free.

Heritage Park comprises a history museum and restored Floridian community. Open Mon.–Fri. 9am–4pm; Sat. 10am–4pm; Sun. 1–5pm. 11909 125th St N, Largo. (813 448 2474).

Hillsborough County Museum features Florida's natural and human history and displays various objets d'art. Open Tues.–Sat. 9am–5pm; Sun. 2.30–5.30pm. 1101 E. River Cove, Tampa. (813 932 8719).

Museum of Fine Arts houses a wide variety of works of art from round the world. Open Tues.–Sat. 10am–5pm; Sun.

Hemingway House, Key West

Villa Vizcaya, Miami

Bellm's Cars and Music of Yesterday, Sarasota

1–5pm. 255 Beach Dr., N, St. Petersburg. (813 896 2667). Donation expected.

Railroad Station Museum devotes itself to railroad history. Open Tues.–Sat. 10am–12pm; Sun. 2–4pm. 341 Main St, Dunedin. (813 733 1291).

Ringling Museums include the Ringling mansion and art collection, the Asolo Theater and the Museum of the Circus. Open Mon.–Fri. 9am–7pm; Sat. 9am–5pm; Sun. 11am–6pm. On US 41 N, Sarasota. (813 355 5101). Admission charge.

St. Petersburg Historical Museum traces the history of the area. Open Mon.–Sat. 11am–5pm; Sun. 1–5pm. 335 2nd Ave NE, St. Petersburg. (813 894 1052). Admission charge.

Science Center of Pinellas County outlines the area's natural history with botanical and geological displays. Open daily 9am–4pm. 7701 22nd Ave N, St. Petersburg. (813 342 8691). Free.

South Florida Museum and Bishop Planetarium combines medicine, history and science. Open Tues.–Sat. 10am–5pm; Sun. 1–5pm; late hours Fri., Sat. 7–10pm. 201 10th St W, Bradenton. (813 746 4131). Admission charge.

Tampa Bay Art Center exhibits paintings and pre-Columbian artifacts. Open Tues.–Fri. 10am–5pm; Sat. 10am–3pm; Sun. 1–5pm. 320 North Blvd, Tampa. (813 253 5346). Free.

Tampa Junior Museum has plenty of touch-and-try exhibits for youngsters. Open Mon.–Fri. 9am–5pm. 1908 Dekle Ave, Tampa. (813 258 4691). Free.

(Northwest)

Air Force Armaments Museum features historic aircraft and airborne ordnance from World War I onwards. Open Tues.–Sat. 9am–4.15pm; Sun., Mon. 12.30–4.15pm. East Gate, Eglin Air Force Base, Valparaiso. (904 882 4062). Free.

Black Archives Center is a major museum of Afro-American history. Open 7 days a week 9am–4pm. Part of Florida A & M (Agricultural and Mechanical) University, Tallahassee. (904 599 3020). Free.

Cedar Key State Museum displays the town's cultural and natural history. Open daily 9am–5pm. Off State 24, on Whitman Drive, Cedar Key. (904 543 5350). Admission charge.

Constitution Convention Museum commemorates the signing of Florida's first constitution and shows Port St. Joe's history. Open daily 9am–5pm. 200 Allen Memorial Way, Port St. Joe. (904 227 8131). Admission charge.

Florida State University Art Gallery features changing exhibitions of contemporary American art. Open Mon.–Fri. 10am–4pm; weekends 1–4pm. In the Fine Arts Building on W. Tennessee St, Tallahassee. (904 644 6836). Free.

Forest Capital Museum has presentations of Florida's forestry industry and ecology. Open daily 9am–5pm. 204 Forest Dr., Perry. (904 584 3227). Admission charge.

Good Life Showboat is a unique maritime museum. Open daily 10am–5pm. 5128 W. US 98, Panama City. (904 763 9175). Admission charge.

Historical Society Museum displays Indian history and Florida's pioneer days. Open Tues.–Sat. 11am–4pm; Sun. 2.30–5.30pm. 115 Westview Ave, Tallahassee. (904 678 2615). Free.

Indian Temple Mound Museum is a treasure house of the area's 10,000-year Indian history. Open Tues.–Sat. 11am–4pm; Sun. 1–4pm; late hours Thurs. 6–8pm. 139 Miracle Strip Parkway, Fort Walton Beach. (904 243 6521). Admission charge.

John Gorrie Museum, on 6th St, Apalachicola, shows refrigeration in the 19th century. Open 7 days a week 9am–5pm. (904 653 3483). Admission charge.

Junior Museum of Bay County appeals to children and has continually changing exhibits. Open Tues.–Fri. 9am–12pm and 1.30–5pm. 1731 Jenks Ave, Panama City. (904 785 8722). Free.

LeMoyne Art Foundation has a collection of paintings, sculpture and ceramics. Open Tues.–Sat. 10am–5pm; Sun. 2–5pm. 125 Gadsden St, Tallahassee. (904 222 8800). Free.

Museum of Florida History displays Florida's history from prehistoric times to present day and includes extensive Spanish treasure exhibits. Open Mon.–Sat. 9am–4.30pm; Sun. 1–4.30pm. In the R.A. Gray Archives, Library and Museum Bldg, S.Bronough St, Tallahassee. (904 488 1484). Free.

Naval Aviation Museum includes displays of 60 historic aircraft plus various types of airborne ordnance. Open daily 9am–5pm. Enquire at the NAS gate, Pensacola. (904 452 3604). Free.

Pensacola Art Center houses contemporary art works and graphics. Open Tues.–Sat. 10am–5pm. 407 S. Jefferson St, Pensacola. (904 432 6247). Free.

Pensacola Historical Museum displays artifacts and antiques depicting the area's history. Open Tues.–Sat. 9am–5.30pm. 405 S. Adams St, Pensacola. (904 433 1559). Free.

San Marcos de Apalache Historic Site is an interpretive center with Indian history. Open daily 9am–5pm. St. Marks. (904 925 6216). Admission charge.

Stephen Foster Center illustrates the life of the composer who made the Suwannee River famous in song. Open daily 8.30am–5.30pm. Three miles from Interstate 75, White Springs. (904 397 2192). Admission charge.

T.T. Wentworth Jr. Museum is devoted completely to local history. Open weekends 2–6pm. 8382 Palafox Highway, Pensacola. (904 476 3443). Free.

Tallahassee Junior Museum shows how life was on a 'cracker' (pioneer) farm of the 1880s. Open Tues.–Sat. 9am–5pm; Sun. 2–5pm. 3945 Museum Dr., Tallahassee. (904 576 1636). Admission charge.

West Florida Museum of History features artifacts showing the history of the area. Open Mon.–Sat. 10am–5.30pm. 205 E. Zaragoza St, Pensacola. (904 432 6717). Donation expected.

PARKS AND FORESTS

(Northeast)

Anastasia Recreation Area St. Augustine Beach, on State A1A. A popular oceanside park, covering more than 1000 acres of land, it includes dunes, beaches, a lagoon and the site where the Spanish quarried the coquina rock used to build Castillo de San Marcos. Facilities for camping, picnicking, swimming, saltwater fishing, boating and nature trails.

Bulow Plantation Ruins Historic Site 8mi. N of Ormond Beach. A 109-acre park with a museum, nature trails, freshwater fishing and picnicking facilities. Ruins of the sugar mill are all that remain of the early 19th-century plantation.

Faver-Dykes 15mi. S of St. Augustine, on highway E of US 1. Woodlands and marsh brimming with bird life extend over 752 acres overlooking the Matanzas River and Pellicer Creek. There are facilities for camping, picnicking, boating, saltwater fishing plus nature trails.

Flagler Beach Recreation Area on State A1A at Flagler Beach. A 145-acre park near the spot where French Huguenot, Jean Ribaut, landed in 1562. There are camping, saltwater fishing, picnicking, swimming, boating, skin and scuba diving facilities.

Fort Clinch Fernandina Beach, on State A1A. One of a chain of masonry forts along the Atlantic coast. Construction was begun in 1847 and in 1861 it was seized (still unfinished) by Confederate troops. Abandoned to Union troops in 1862, it was used as a prison for the rest of the Civil War. There are guided tours, a museum, and special interpretive activities take place on the first Sunday of every month.

Recreational facilities include camping, picnicking, swimming, saltwater fishing, boating, skin and scuba diving.

Ichetucknee Springs Fort White, on State 47. A 2241-acre woodland park along the Ichetucknee River. Springs feed a 3½-mile stretch of the river used for tubing (inner tube float trips). Facilities also for swimming, skin and scuba diving and picnicking.

Little Talbot Island 17mi. NE of Jacksonville, on State A1A. A 2500-acre island park surrounded by the Atlantic, Fort George River and Nassau Sound. Facilities for camping, picnicking, swimming, fishing, boating, skin and scuba diving.

Mike Roess Gold Head 6mi. NE of Keystone Heights, on State 21. This 1414-acre park contains a ravine and flowing stream. A nature trail winds through the ravine and family cabins may be rented within the park confines. The park also contains three lakes and the remains of an old dam and mill. Facilities for camping, picnicking, swimming, saltwater fishing, skin and scuba diving; paddle boat, canoe and bicycle rentals.

O'Leno 20mi. S of Lake City, on US 41. A 5898-acre park on the Santa Fe River which flows underground for three miles within the park. There are sinkholes, hardwood hammock, river swamp and a suspension bridge over the river. Facilities for camping, picnicking, swimming, boating and freshwater fishing plus a number of nature trails.

Osceola National Forest, E of Lake City on US 90, embraces the Olustee monument commemorating the only significant Civil War battle fought on Florida soil. The forest's popular recreation area is Ocean Pond, a lake that offers excellent swimming, fishing and boating. There are also camping and picnicking spots.

Ravine State Gardens off Twigg St, Palatka. A 182-acre landscaped park boasting literally hundreds of thousands of azaleas and other ornamental plants on the banks of natural ravines which plunge to a depth of 70–120 ft. Nature trails and picnic facilities are added attractions.

Washington Oaks State Gardens 3mi. S of Marineland, on State A1A. Once a plantation, this 340-acre estate is bounded by the Atlantic and the Intracoastal Waterway. Among native and exotic plants are pomegranate and guava trees and persimmon. A small museum, nature trails and facilities for picnicking and saltwater fishing are also to be found here.

(Central East Coast)

Blue Springs State Park 2mi. W of

Orange City, off Interstate 4 and US 17.
There are nature trails and facilities for
canoeing, freshwater fishing, scuba diving, camping and swimming. In winter sea
cows, or manatee, live here.

Fort Pierce Inlet Recreation Area
4mi. E of Fort Pierce, off State A1A. A
340-acre park with facilities for picnicking, swimming, boating and saltwater
fishing. Also at Fort Pierce is Pepper Park-
St. Lucie Museum Recreation Area which
includes a lovely white sandy beach and a
958-acre preserve abundant with wildlife.
Guided tours are available and the area
also offers nature trails and facilities for
picnicking, swimming, fishing, boating,
skin and scuba diving.

Jonathan Dickinson 13mi. S of Stuart,
on US 1. A 10,284-acre park encompassing dense pine forests and part of the wild
Loxahatchee River. There are conducted
tours of the area which was named for a
Quaker who was shipwrecked near Hobe
Sound, captured by the Indians but, surprisingly, not killed. There are nature
trails, facilities for camping, picnicking,
swimming, boating and both saltwater and
freshwater fishing. Bikes, boats and canoes are available for rent.

Sebastian Inlet on State A1A. A 578-
acre recreation area that includes the
McLarty Museum on the site of salvage
camps set up by survivors of a Spanish
treasure fleet sunk in a hurricane of 1715.
Facilities for boating, skin and scuba diving, picnicking, surfing and saltwater fishing. A good place, too, for birdwatching.

Tomoka 3mi. N of Ormond Beach. A
914-acre park at the confluence of the
Halifax and Tomoka rivers, formerly site
of an Indian village. There are guided
tours, nature trails and a museum. Canoes,
boats and bikes can be rented and you can
camp, picnic or fish.

(Southeast)

Bahia Honda Bahia Honda Key, on US
1. Florida's most southerly park covers
276 acres. Its main attraction is palm-
fringed beach which edges both the Atlantic Ocean and the Gulf of Mexico. A good
place for swimming, skin and scuba diving
or snorkeling (instruction available).
There are also facilities for camping, boating, picnicking and saltwater fishing.

Bill Baggs Cape Florida Key Biscayne,
off US 1. A 406-acre recreational area
which includes Cape Florida Lighthouse,
the oldest building in south Florida. Tape
recorder tours of the lighthouse and museum are available. In addition to a vast
beach area there are nature trails and
facilities for picnicking, boating, skin and
scuba diving and saltwater fishing.

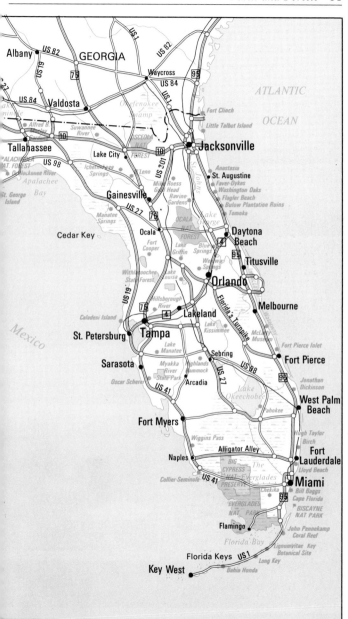

Anhinga Trail

Airboat

Everglades National Park (Background)

Biscayne National Park comprises 4200 acres of land in the Upper Keys plus 92,000 acres of submerged land and water in Biscayne Bay and the Atlantic. There are guided tours of the area and also boat trips from Convey Point to Elliott Key. Facilities for camping, picnicking, swimming, fishing, snorkeling and scuba diving plus nature trails.

Chekika 11mi. NW of Homestead, at 24200 SW 160th St. A 640-acre park with artesian springs which have a daily water flow of three million gallons. Facilities for camping, picnicking, swimming, freshwater fishing and nature trails.

Everglades National Park A protected tract of marshland and fragmented coastline covering 1.4 million acres, or 2120 square miles. It is feasible to see only part of such vastness and you need to slacken pace and take time to adjust to the unique wilderness atmosphere here.

From Miami take US 1 south to Florida City, then 9mi. of State 27. Watch for road signs indicating the way to the park. At the main entrance there is a Visitor Center where you can pick up a free map of the park, packed with information.

The Everglades was a part of Florida unexplored until the middle of the 19th century when US troops were sent in search of the Seminole Indians. Efforts to reclaim the swamp began in 1903 and in 1905 the Everglades Drainage District was established.

With its wealth of bird and animal life, vegetation and waterways, it is one of the state's greatest natural treasures. A conspicuous feature is the number of 'hammocks' (small islands of hardwood trees and shrubs) which dot the swamps. Ponds and deep channels, scattered with tiny islands, crisscross the Glades.

While live oak, coco plum and custard apple trees often create dense thickets on the higher ground, the cypress is the most common tree on the lower ground. Big Cypress Swamp (not part of the park but contiguous to it) of Collier County is the largest of its kind in Florida, and 'Old Senator' at Longwood is a Florida cypress said to date back over 3500 years. The Glades are also famous for their abundance of orchids and some really enormous specimens have been found here.

The creature most associated with the Everglades is the alligator. In summer alligators move into the coastal sections of Florida Bay and the Gulf of Mexico. A good way to watch them is at any of the ponds along the Anhinga Trail. Other animals you might catch sight of include black bears, panthers, wildcats, otters and raccoons. There are 300 varieties of birds and more than 600 varieties of fish.

Swamp buggy

A hammock in the Everglades (Background)

The 100-mile inland waterway is excellent for canoes or other small boats in the hands of the adventurous as the trail winds through creeks, rivers and open bays. Numerous well-known walking trails range from half a mile to much, much more. The Anhinga Trail, named for a native bird, is 1½ miles along a raised boardwalk over sawgrass marshland. Adjacent is the Gumbo Limbo Trail, named for a tropical tree, which winds for half a mile through a hammock. The Pineland Trail extends for 6½ miles and offers a good chance of spotting orchid varieties and the white-tailed deer. Best view of the sawgrass marsh is from the observation tower located on the 12½ mile Pa-hay-okee Trail. From here you can see Mahogany Hammock which contains the largest mahogany tree in the US.

Fresh and salt water mingle at Nine Mile Pond (in reality, 26½ miles). A boardwalk leads into the brackish waters of the unique mangrove swamp at West Lake, starting point of a favorite canoe trail. Picnic facilities can be found at Paurotis Pond and there are campsites at Long Key where, in winter, campfire programs are conducted.

Main tourist section is at Flamingo which has its own lodge and marina as well as campsites. All kinds of boats may be rented here for fishing expeditions, houseboating, or merely a spin in an outboard. The easiest way to enjoy the region is on an organized cruise: passing Coot Bay, traveling along Buttonwood Canal, visiting Tarpon Creek and reaching Cape Sable, the southernmost point of continental USA. Passengers go ashore here and take the Wilderness Train through mangrove forests and Snake Bight Trail. An alternative method of travel is a tram tour starting at Shark Valley and lasting about 1½ hours. Sightseeing boat tours of the Ten Thousand Islands inland areas start near Everglades City and last from 1½ to 2½ hours

Fishing is possible in a host of park areas and many trails are suited to cycling.

Hugh Taylor Birch Fort Lauderdale, on State A1A. A 180-acre park which includes Atlantic beachfront, inland waterway and lagoons. It features a 3-mile train ride and nature trails and has facilities for picnicking, swimming, boating, skin and scuba diving plus saltwater fishing.

John Pennekamp Coral Reef Key Largo, on US 1. The first underwater state park in the US, covering 52,722 acres of offshore water and 2289 acres of land. It is home to a multitude of tropical fish and some 50 kinds of living coral. Ideal for snorkelers (instruction available), skin and scuba divers, though the easier way is to take a glass-bottom boat tour of the reef. Marine life includes barracuda, giant sea turtles and sharks.

Boat and canoe rentals are available. Water trails near the shore wind into the mangrove swamp and are well suited to canoeing. A roped-off area along the beach can be used by swimmers and there are places to picnic. The park has a number of nature trails and campsites equipped with tables and grills, but this park is so popular that advance reservations are usually necessary. For information call (305) 451 1621.

Lignumvitae Key Botanical Site off US 1 near Islamorada. A 478-acre park off Lower Matecumbe Key, it also encompasses Shell Key. Facilities for boating, skin and scuba diving and nature trails.

Lloyd Beach Recreation Area just S of Fort Lauderdale, off State A1A. A 243-acre park with facilities for picnicking, swimming, boating, skin and scuba diving, saltwater fishing; also canoe rentals.

Long Key at Islamorada, on US 1. An 849-acre park in the middle of the Florida Keys near Layton. Particularly noted for its excellent saltwater fishing, there are also facilities for camping, picnicking, boating, swimming, skin and scuba diving. Snorkeling instruction is available and there are nature trails through the area.

Pahokee Recreation Area on US 441. A 30-acre park, above Hoover Dike on Lake Okeechobee, with camping, picnicking, swimming, boating and freshwater fishing facilities.

(Central Florida)

Highlands Hammock 6mi. W of Sebring, off US 27-98. A 3800-acre wildlife preserve where you can camp, picnic, bike or walk along a nature trail. There is a museum and guided tours of the preserve are available.

Lake Griffin Recreation Area NE of Leesburg, off US 27-441. A lakeside park on one of Florida's largest lakes, with facilities for camping, picnicking, boating, freshwater fishing and nature trails.

Lake Kissimmee, 18mi. E of Lake Wales, used to be ranchland. There are nature trails through the 5000 acres, guided tours of the historic features, a picnic area, an 1876 'cow camp' and opportunities for fishing and boating.

Lake Louisa 7mi. SW of Clermont, on State 561, comprises 1790 acres where you can picnic, swim or go freshwater fishing.

Ocala National Forest covers 286,000 acres between the Oklawaha and St. Johns rivers, east of Ocala. Nicknamed the 'Big

Scrub' because of its vast acreage of sand pine, it maintains one of the state's largest herds of deer and is a year-round fisherman's paradise. There are two recreational areas: Juniper Springs in Marion County and Alexander Springs in Lake County.

Juniper Springs is 26 miles E of Ocala on State 40. The springs themselves are the main feature, pouring out over eight million gallons of water daily at a constant 72° temperature. Facilities include hiking trails, canoeing, swimming and camping. Alexander Springs lies 16 miles N of Eustis, E of State 19. Some 76 million gallons of water per day flow out here at a temperature of 72°. Game fishing is good at Spring Creek and other facilities include swimming, boating, picnicking and camping.

Wekiwa Springs, E of Apopka on State 436, is a 6000-acre park for family recreation. There are picnic facilities, swimming, boating, scuba diving, nature trails, boat rentals and youth campsites.

(West Coast)

Caladesi Island Park 2mi. offshore of Dunedin and reached by ferry or private boat from the city marina. No vehicles are allowed on the island, a refuge for wading and shore birds. Its white sand beaches on the Gulf of Mexico are superb and one can go boating, fishing or shelling from there.

Collier-Seminole Park 17mi. S of Naples, on US 41. A 6423-acre park where Big Cypress Swamp joins the Everglades. According to history, this was the last refuge of the Seminole Indians. There is a museum here, nature trails and facilities for camping, picnicking and saltwater fishing.

Fort Cooper Park, Inverness, has historic items and there are 707 acres in which to picnic, fish or swim.

Hillsborough River Park 6mi. SW of Zephyrhills, off US 301. A 2810-acre family recreation area not far from Tampa. Bird and plant life abound within its forest and around its spring-fed river. A swinging bridge leads to nature trails. There are facilities for swimming, picnicking, boating, camping and freshwater fishing; canoes and other boats can be rented here.

Lake Manatee Recreation Area 14mi. E of Bradenton, on State 64. A 556-acre lakeside park where you can picnic, swim, boat, fish or take to a nature trail.

Myakka River Park 17mi. E of Sarasota, on State 72. A 28,857-arce preserve where Spanish moss hangs from wide-spreading oaks. The name is thought to be a variant of the Timucuan word *mayaca* meaning large. With its river and lakes, this preserve is particularly noted for a wide variety of bird and wildlife. Family cabins may be rented here and there are also campsites. Facilities for picnicking and freshwater fishing; boats and bikes may be rented. There's a museum and nature trails and guided tours of the preserve are available.

Oscar Scherer Recreation Area 2mi. S of Osprey, on US 41. Facilities for saltwater fishing, boating, camping and picnicking; canoes and bicycles can be rented here; also nature trails.

Wiggins Pass 6mi. S of Bonita Springs, on County road 901 off US 41. A 166-acre site on the north end of a barrier spit separated from the mainland by mangrove swamps and tidal creeks. This is a popular nesting area for sea turtles and it also attracts large numbers of shore and wading birds. Beachside swimming is possible as well as boating and saltwater fishing.

Withlacoochee State Forest has three tracts SE of Brooksville. A 113,000-acre area of tall pines where you can camp, ride, hike and fish. Swimming and hunting are possible in certain designated sections.

(Northwest)

Alfred B. Maclay State Gardens 5mi. N of Tallahassee, on US 319. A 251-acre area, on the shores of Lake Hall, where formal gardens are combined with recreational activities. The garden is a floral masterpiece with the emphasis on azaleas and camellias but there are also rare native trees and plants such as the Torreya and silver bell. Best season to see blooms is Jan.–Apr. There are guided tours of Maclay House museum. In the recreational section there are nature trails plus facilities for picnicking, swimming, boating and fishing.

Apalachicola National Forest is the most extensive in Florida, lying west of Tallahassee and spreading to the Apalachicola River. It covers parts of Leon, Wakulla, Franklin and Liberty Counties and encompasses four state parks and recreation areas plus the Ochlockonee River. Wildlife, including black bear and panther, is plentiful. There are excellent spots for fishing, swimming and picnicking and several campsites, best of which is at Silver Lake Recreation Area, reached by turning S off State 20 and following State 260 for three miles into the forest. Regulated hunting in some sections.

Basin Bayou 7mi. W of Freeport, on State 20. A 287-acre area facing Basin Bayou and Choctawhatchee Bay. Facilities for camping, picnicking, boating and both salt and freshwater fishing.

Blackwater River 15mi. NE of Milton, on US 90. A 360-acre park on Blackwater

River in Blackwater River State Forest. There are nature trails and facilities for camping, picnicking, swimming, boating and freshwater fishing.

Dead Lakes Recreation Area 4mi. N of Wewahitchka, on State 71. A 41-acre park named for the numerous dead cypress, oak and pine trees drowned by the natural overflow from the Chipola River. Facilities for camping, picnicking, boating, freshwater fishing plus nature trails.

Falling Waters Recreation Area 3mi. S of Chipley, off State 77A. A 154-acre vacation park round a waterfall. It offers an 80-ft sinkhole, nature trails, camping, picnicking and swimming facilities.

Florida Caverns 3mi. N of Marianna, on State 167. A 1783-acre park surrounding a limestone cavern full of stalagmites and stalactites. The natural bridge here is the one crossed, during the 1818 Indian campaign, by General Andrew Jackson unaware that many Indians had taken refuge in the caverns below.

A popular park, it boasts camping and picnicking areas, nature trails, a nine-hole golf course, an archeological museum and also has facilities for swimming, boating, skin and scuba diving and fishing.

Fred Gannon Rocky Bayou 3mi. E of Niceville, on State 20. A 622-acre park within Eglin Air Force Base. It contains nature trails and has facilities for camping, picnicking, swimming, boating and saltwater fishing.

Grayton Beach Recreation Area on State 30A. 356 acres of pine woodlands with white beaches and freshwater lakes. Facilities for camping, picnicking, swimming, boating, skin and scuba diving, fishing and nature trails.

Maclay State Gardens (see Alfred B. Maclay, p.57)

Manatee Springs 6 mi. W of Chiefland, on State 320. A 2074-acre area surrounding one of the most beautiful springs in the country. 49,000 gallons per minute pour into the Suwannee River. Facilities for camping, picnicking, swimming, skin and scuba diving and freshwater fishing. Boats, canoes and bikes can be rented and there are nature trails.

Ochlockonee River 4mi. S of Sopchoppy, on US 319. A 392-acre park bounded by two rivers and scattered with small ponds. Facilities for camping, picnicking, swimming, boating, freshwater fishing plus nature trails.

St. Andrews Recreation Area 3mi. E of Panama City Beach, on State 392. The 1062-acre park contains wide beaches, sand dunes, a restored 'cracker' (pioneer) turpentine still, museum and nature trails. Also facilities for camping, picnicking, swimming, boating, skin and scuba diving and saltwater fishing.

St. George Island State Park off US 98, near Apalachicola; on the east end of St. George Island. A 1882-acre area with a beach, boardwalks, observation platforms and boat ramps on the bay. The picnic area has rest rooms and there is a camping area.

Suwannee River 13mi. W of Live Oak, on US 90. A 1831-acre park where oaks are entwined with Spanish moss and cypress trees line the banks of the river made famous in Stephen Foster's song. You'll find nature trails and facilities for camping, picnicking, swimming, boating and freshwater fishing.

Three Rivers Recreation Area 1mi. N of Sneads, on State 271. 834 acres on the edge of forest and lake, offering nature trails plus camping, picnicking, boating and freshwater fishing.

Torreya between Bristol and Greensboro, on State 271 off State 12. A 1063-acre vacation and botanical park named for a tree which grows only in a 20-mile radius of the park. Guided tours are available and there are facilities for camping, picnicking, freshwater fishing plus nature trails.

Grayton Beach Recreation Area

THE NORTHEAST

The northeast is the state's most historic area for it was here that the first European settlers established themselves. The fortresses and weathered structures which survive from Spanish times create a permanent link with the past, and the restoration of old districts is a project very much on the minds of today's town councils. After all, the nation's oldest city, St. Augustine, is located in this region.

The history of the northeast is a major drawing card and numerous historic sites and points of interest help to preserve it, but the area is also becoming noted for its 'Deep South' hospitality while special events give it a year-round festive air.

The natural highlights of the land are a predominant feature. Oil magnate Henry Flagler recognized this when he developed the resort facilities that were to become the first of a string extending right down Florida's east coast. Flagler Beach is named for him, of course, and other early beach resorts include Fernandina, Jacksonville, Atlantic and Neptune. They are all quite different in character, ranging as they do from rocky shores and dune-ringed islands to beaches so hard-packed that cars can drive on them. Thanks to the Gulf Stream the waters are warm.

In this corner of the state water plays a key role since the northeast encompasses the St. Johns, St. Marys, Suwannee and Santa Fe rivers as well as countless lakes. It means that outdoor activities are limitless. Fishermen can catch trophy-sized fish and have the choice of saltwater or freshwater fishing. Canoeists will find plenty of outfitters to supply them and even novices needn't be afraid to try the sport as there are runs to suit all stages of expertise.

Within the northeast there are fifteen state parks, the Osceola National Forest and seven game management areas, under the supervision of the state game and fish commission, which offer ideal camping and picnicking sites. The outdoors enthusiast can choose from a plethora of nature trails or conducted walks, overnight backpacking or wildlife study rambles. There are organized outings at Little Talbot Island State Park, San Felasco Hammock State Preserve and Payne's Prairie State Preserve to name just three.

Sport is an important element here. A number of major professional golf and tennis tournaments are held annually and other professional, collegiate and amateur events take place throughout the year. Playing the game rather than watching it

poses no problem either. Amelia Island and Sawgrass golf courses are among the country's most challenging but there are lots of other private and public golf courses for holiday enjoyment and there are just as many tennis courts.

Three kennel clubs in the region offer greyhound racing ten months of the year while Gator Bowl Festival and Football Classic (Jacksonville) is a highlight in December. Fetes and festivals take place somewhere every month – from craft fairs to rodeos and art shows to regattas. City sightseeing is best in Jacksonville and St. Augustine where there are museums, good shopping and dining facilities and restored historic quarters.

The region's extensive fishing fleets ensure that fresh seafood appears on countless menus. Look out for the April Blessing of the Fleet and Catfish Festival in St. Augustine.

Where to stay? In recent years accommodations have much improved their standards of service. Besides the Hiltons, Howard Johnsons and Ramadas, the less well-known names offer a happy alternative. The Kenwood Inn, built in the late 1800s, is small and cozy, furnished with family antiques and located in St. Augustine's historic district. Rooms at the 1735 House on Amelia Island are all suites sleeping up to six people. Guests at The Inn at Baymeadows in the Jacksonville area get club membership privileges to the Bay Meadows Golf Club next door. Tiny Bailey House at Fernandina Beach is filled with objects from the turn of the century.

By way of contrast, modern resorts include Amelia Island Plantation where the emphasis is on golf and tennis and a 44-ft sailing ketch is available for charter. Sawgrass Resort in Ponte Vedra Beach has studio villas at the Beach Club and offers a shuttle service between resorts in street-legal golf carts.

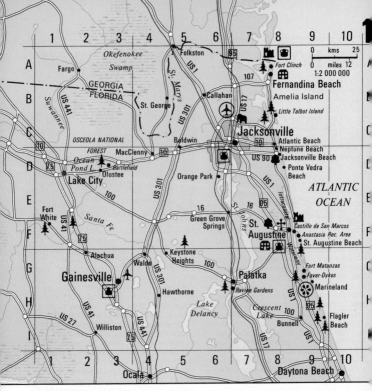

Fernandina Beach   A8

(pop. 6955) A colorful, quaint, historic town located on the northwestern shore of Amelia Island. Once an active port on account of its natural harbor, it now relies on shrimp factories and pulp mills, although it is the exceptional beach which attracts visitors here.

In 1686, when the island was known as Santa Maria, there was a Spanish post here on a hillside just north of today's town. It was captured (and its mission destroyed) in 1702 when South Carolina's governor, James Moore, attacked the island with an English force and Indian allies. So many subsequent attacks took place that by 1730 the island was deserted.

General James Oglethorpe re-established a post here in 1735. He found the island so beautiful that he renamed it in honor of George II's sister, Princess Amelia. Since Florida was loyal to the British Crown, a British fort was built on the island's northern end at the start of the Revolutionary War. As the tide turned against the British in the colonies, large numbers of Tories came south to the island, but they were forced to leave when Florida was returned to Spain in 1783. The Spanish government granted a large tract of land to Don Domingo Fernandez, which included a village named Fernandina in his honor. Situated as it was just across the American border, it became a haunt of pirates and smugglers during the early 19th century.

Of historic note today is **Fort Clinch**, one in a chain of US masonry forts built along the Atlantic coast. Construction was begun in 1847 but never completed. The fort was seized by Confederate troops in 1861 and abandoned in 1862 to Union troops who used it as a prison. There are guided tours of the fort and its museum and interpretive activities take place the first Sunday of every month. You can swim, picnic or boat in the grounds.

In downtown Fernandina Beach see the restored 20-block **Historic District** which includes Centre Street, surrounding Victorian houses and Florida's oldest saloon, the Palace, which has been in continuous operation since 1903.

Accommodations include small Bailey House and Amelia Island Plantation which sponsors seasonal events.

Fort Clinch, Fernandina Beach

French Huguenot, Jean Ribaut, landed in the 16th century at what is now the **Flagler Beach Recreation Area** which offers camping, fishing, picnicking, swimming and boating.

Gainesville   G3

(pop. 72,100) A college town located midway between the Atlantic Ocean and the Gulf of Mexico. It became an education center when an academy was started here, in 1867, forming the nucleus of the State Seminary for the region east of the Suwannee. It was consolidated as the University of Florida in 1905. As one might expect, much activity revolves round the campus, although agriculture and light industry are also important to Gainesville. Of particular note is the University of Florida Art Gallery which features traveling exhibits and art displays by students and faculty.

When De Soto marched through the area in 1539, it was known as Potano Province, a name that was changed to Alachua when the Creek Indians took possession under British rule in 1763. The white settlement known as Hog Town, which grew up round the trading post here in 1830, was renamed Gainesville in 1853 in honor of General Edmund P. Gaines, one of the leaders in the Seminole Wars. See the historic exhibits in the Florida State Museum which has anthropological displays including a reconstructed Florida cave.

Jacksonville   C7

(pop. 539,000) The largest, most commercial town in the region, the banks of its St. Johns River are lined with skyscrapers. An important timber and tobacco center, it

was also one of the earliest settlements and French and Spanish forts still survive. Named for General Andrew Jackson (despite the fact that the nearest he came to the town was the Suwannee River), Jacksonville's streets were laid out in 1822, though even by 1830 the population could muster only 300 heads.

The city was incorporated in 1832 but the charter was repealed in 1840, leaving Jacksonville without a city government for 11 months. By 1842 it was prospering. Schooners filled its harbor and seafarers crowded Bay Street's bars, gambling houses and brothels.

At the start of the Civil War, sympathies lay with the south and when the state joined the Confederacy, blockade runners made Jacksonville their base. It became a popular winter resort city after 1863 when the first theater and several large hotels like the St. James were built. When it opened in 1869, the St. James was referred to as the Fifth Avenue Hotel of Florida and, 14 years later, it was the first Florida hotel to install electric lights.

A fire in 1901 swept through 148 blocks destroying 2000 buildings, but subsequent rebuilding gave the city a bold new face. See Cummer Gallery of Art which houses one of the southeast's finest collections of modern art. Contemporary art is also prominent at the Jacksonville Art Museum while the Jacksonville Museum of Arts and Sciences has displays of special interest for the young. The Alexander Brest Planetarium (within the museum) features astronomy shows and weekend cosmic concerts which combine lasers and rock or classical music.

Jacksonville has a number of theaters,

its own ballet troupe and a symphony orchestra with a year-round schedule. Its 61-acre Jacksonville Zoological Park features 700 exotic and native animals in natural habitats. Friendship Park and Marina overlooks downtown Jacksonville and provides boat slips for overnight dockage. Hotels include a Sheraton at St. Johns Place on the St. Johns River, across from the downtown area, Hilton, Ramada and Howard Johnson.

Jacksonville Beach is Jacksonville's resort center where Kathryn Abbey Hannah Park offers 1½ miles of beach, campsites, nature trails and 60 acres of stocked fishing lakes. Fishing is also popular off the beach's pier and boardwalk. Hotels along the oceanfront include a Holiday Inn and Ramada. Just south, at **Ponte Vedra Beach**, Sawgrass Resort is a villa/hotel complex.

Jacksonville

Lake City   D1

(pop. 10,575) One of early Florida's influential towns. Between 1883 and 1905 it was the seat of the State Agricultural College. Today it encompasses part of the Osceola National Forest and Ocean Pond, a large lake noted for its excellent swimming and fishing. The **Olustee Battlefield** here is a monument commemorating the biggest battle fought in Florida during the course of the Civil War. Lake City was originally known as Alligator, the name of a Seminole chief who ruled a nearby Indian village.

Palatka   G7

(pop. 9444) The town has been an important shipping center since the 1800s and still is one of the largest lumber shipping centers in the south. It was a thriving tourist resort in the days immediately following the Civil War when river traffic was at its zenith. It takes its name from the Indian word *Pilaklikaha* (crossing over) given to the trading post established on the river in 1821. Main tourist attraction today is **Ravine Gardens**, a 182-acre botanical park particularly noted for its azaleas. Fed by springs and spanned by suspension bridges, the ravine's creek frequently widens into pools blanketed with lilies and other flowering plants. Nature trails wind along the steep slopes and through the ravine. The town is at its most colorful in March when the annual Azalea Festival takes place.

St. Augustine   F8

(pop. 12,352) The nation's oldest city, its site was chosen for strategic reasons by the Spanish in 1565. Founded by Don Pedro Menendez de Aviles, it served as Florida's capital for centuries. It was Ponce de Leon who discovered the area on St. Augustine's day in 1513 – hence the name. The town became the Spanish military headquarters for North America and for many years its governors manned forts and patrolled the coast to ward off attempts by other nations to set up colonies here.

In fact it was attacked and taken over several times. One of the most severe attacks was mounted by Sir Francis Drake in 1586, though it wasn't until 1763 that the British managed to claim St. Augustine. It enjoyed prosperity under British rule for 20 years by which time the Indians were no longer a menace and great plantations had been established.

In the 1880s Henry Flagler was impressed enough by the small Spanish community to start to develop it as a winter resort; he built two large hotels and extended a railroad southwards. It wasn't until after 1900, however, that residential districts grew and the population was swelled by European immigrants, particularly Minorcans.

San Augustin Antiguo is the town's restored historic quarter and it looks as it did in the 18th century, with costumed craftsmen demonstrating the crafts of that era. See the Oldest House, much the same as it was during Spanish colonial times. There are tours of this two-story structure, believed to have been built in 1509. (Open 9am–6pm.) The Oldest Schoolhouse on George Street was also built during the first Spanish occupation. Made of red cedar and cypress joined together by wooden pegs, it contains museum items and is also open for viewing. Oldest Store on Artillery Lane would have been a popular meeting place for the community in the 1800s. Costumed staff show you round the turn-of-the-century general store which houses such rarities as cigar-store Indians and the Edison Victrola.

There are more than 70 sites of interest in historic St. Augustine. Among them are: Casa de Hidalgo, built by the Spanish and furnished in the style of early 17th-century Spain. De Mesa Sanchez House, an old Spanish inn restored to its 1831 condition. Flagler College, housed in the

San Augustin Antiguo

Oldest House in the USA

Castillo de San Marcos

former Ponce de Leon Hotel built by Henry Flagler in 1888, and Flagler Memorial Presbyterian Church built by Flagler in 1889. The ornate St. Augustine Cathedral was built by the Spanish in the 1790s. The site of the founding of the town is known as the Nombre de Dios where America's first mission was also founded. You can visit the Shrine of Nuestra Senora de la Leche which has a religious art center, and Fountain of Youth Discovery Park, on Magnolia Avenue, a memorial to Ponce de Leon.

Castillo de San Marcos is North America's oldest masonry fort. The construction of native coquina was begun by the Spanish in 1672 but took 25 years to complete. Visitors can tour the battlements which have special exhibits. **Fort Matanzas**, built in 1742, can also be toured. It is on the site of the bitter 16th-century struggle between French and Spanish colonists that ended in the massacre of 300 French Huguenots.

St. Augustine's historic district may be toured on foot, by carriage or by sightseeing train which travels a seven-mile guided route, stopping at attractions.

Don't miss Museum of Yesterday's Toys (in the historic quarter) with its collection of rare and valuable toys. Fine examples of Tiffany glass can be seen in the Lightner Museum (the former Alcazar Hotel built by Henry Flagler), which also has Victorian glassware, porcelain, bronze

and marble statuary. Zorayda Castle houses an outstanding art collection in what is a re-creation of Spain's famous Alhambra.

Fun museums include the Wax Museum, one of the country's oldest, with over 240 figures, and Ripley's Believe It or Not Museum containing all kinds of oddities. Robert Ripley traveled to 200 countries to collect 750 items now displayed in this museum on San Marco Avenue. In the vicinity are two alligator farms: **Gatorland Alligator Farm** with thousands of crocs and gators, and **St. Augustine Alligator Farm**, the state's oldest attraction – it started operation in 1893 – which has hourly shows featuring alligator wrestling.

One of the most beautiful natural areas is **Faver-Dykes**, 752 acres of woodlands and marsh overlooking Matanzas River and Pellicer Creek. It has nature trails and facilities for camping, fishing, picnicking and boating.

St. Augustine has a wide choice of places to stay including the Monson Motor Lodge (which has a dinner theater) and small Kenwood Inn in the historic area.

A popular oceanside park at St. Augustine Beach is the **Anastasia Recreation Area** with over 1000 acres of hard-packed beaches, dunes and a lagoon. Within the site is the place where the Spaniards quarried the coquina rock used to build Fort San Marcos.

THE CENTRAL EAST COAST

Racing! The one word that best conjures up the central east coast, an area extending from Ormond Beach in the north to Hobe Sound in the south. This region was the birth place of both the Kennedy Space Center, engaged in man's boldest race, and Daytona Beach, famous for its International Speedway.

For more than 80 years, the world's fastest cars have been competing fiercely along this coastline, attracting crowds of enthusiasts in their wake. Early auto magnates wintering here introduced the sport to the area, putting it on the map. Names like Ransom Olds, Henry Ford and Louis Chevrolet established Daytona as a go-ahead, family fun resort with plenty of action, plenty to do. Auto racing has moved from the hard beaches to a track with a world-famous reputation.

Not far to the south, midway down the coast, the space race continues from a triangle of land that was identified on 15th-century maps: Cape Canaveral, the oldest place name in the western hemisphere. Kennedy Space Center allows visitors to get some idea of the inside workings of the Space Program. An $8 million expansion program has doubled facilities at the Center. There is now an additional theater complex housing a 500-seat computerized demonstration auditorium and a 440-seat theater with an IMAX projection system, five stories high with a 70-ft-wide screen. A souvenir shop, food area and an extra 10,000 sq. ft of exhibit space have also been added.

The Visitor Center, just inside the main gate, displays many of the rockets launched along with memorabilia from past missions. And you might well be able to catch an actual space shuttle launch (see also p.18).

The central east coast is not without natural attractions. Merritt Island National Wildlife Refuge lies within the boundaries of the Kennedy Space Center and is a permanent showcase for the flora and fauna of the region. Boat is a particularly pleasant way to discover Florida's wildlife and several operations feature short cruises along the St. Lucie and St. Johns rivers. Birdwatchers will find the best time is winter when this region is home to thousands of species. The annual nesting and egg-laying of the huge sea turtles also takes place here. Pelican Island is a prime nesting spot for the brown pelican and Lake Woodruff near De Land is a refuge for waterfowl.

The area is peppered with campgrounds (from the primitive to luxurious sites catering to motor homes) and boating and fishing facilities. Recreation areas include Sebastian Inlet park and Outdoor Resorts: a campground (with 576 sites) devoted exclusively to recreational vehicles, on both ocean and river frontage along Melbourne's waterfront; it has tennis courts and pool for campers' use.

Many of the area's beaches are quiet and secluded. Others are good for surfing, with holiday bases anywhere from New Smyrna Beach to Cocoa Beach and south to Melbourne. Fishing offers a choice of salt water in the Atlantic or fresh water in rivers like the Banana and the upper reaches of the Indian, both good for trout. Wahoo or dolphin are plentiful in offshore waters and charter fleets can be found at Ormond Beach, Cocoa Beach, Vero Beach, Fort Pierce and Stuart.

All the seashore communities boast a wide range of accommodations to suit all budgets, from Quality Inns and Holiday Inns to resort properties like Sandpiper Bay and renovated 'old ladies' like the Driftwood Inn at Vero Beach or the St. Regis Hotel at Daytona. If your hotel doesn't have its own golf facilities, there are golf clubs like LaCita in Titusville, opened in 1982, with an 18-hole course designed by Lee Trevino.

Brevard County's largest shopping mall is Melbourne Square with major department stores and restaurants. Innumerable festivities are held throughout the year at Daytona. Local specialties to look out for are pompano, red snapper and shrimp, and, of course, citrus fruit, much of which grows along the banks of Indian River.

Cocoa Beach   I6

(pop. 9952) A resort with plenty of

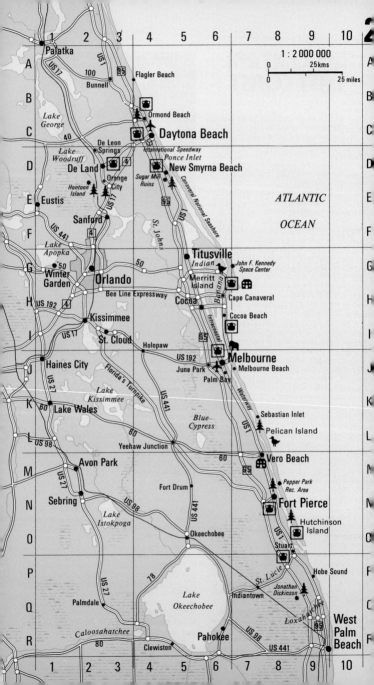

oceanfront hotels, lively bars and restaurants and miles of white sand. See the Patrick Air Force Base Missile Display which has collections of rockets and other space vehicles. Exhibits at the Brevard Art Center and Museum are changed every few weeks and lectures and film shows are often given here. Accommodations include a Holiday Inn and Quality Inn.

The community of **Cocoa** itself lies across the Indian River on the Intracoastal Waterway which connects with the Atlantic. The region is a wealthy fruit producer – oranges have been grown here since 1868. Incorporated as a city in 1895, the name came from the coco plum which grew here in abundance at that time. Today it is a fishing and golfing resort.

Daytona Beach   C4

(pop. 49,300) The central east coast's top resort lies in an area originally inhabited by the Timucuan Indians. Franciscan friars established missions in the region in 1587 but permanent settlement at Daytona didn't begin until 1870 when an Ohio man bought a tract of land and laid out the town, naming it for his own surname of 'Day'.

A New Jersey man built the first proper residence, a log cabin at the corner of First Avenue and North Beach Street. Among the first buildings was Colony House, designed as a hotel to cater to those settlers still without homes. Daytona's population swelled after Flagler extended his railroad south from St. Augustine.

It became associated with motor racing mainly because its ocean beach proved ideal for the sport: 23 miles of hard white sand, 500 ft wide and beaten smooth by incoming tides. The first driver to break the world record on this beach was Alexander Winton in 1903 when he drove his vehicle at 68 mph. Many wealthy racing enthusiasts and car drivers, including John Jacob Astor, William Vanderbilt and Henry Flagler, were attracted to Daytona. Motorists are still allowed to drive along the beach at low tide, but today's big racing events take place at the multi-million-dollar **Daytona International Speedway**. Racing highlights are the Daytona 500 in February and the Firecracker 400 Auto Race in July; there are also the Paul Revere 250 stock car race, the 24 Hour Pepsi Challenge for exotic sport cars, and the Daytona 200 Motorcycle Classic. The Museum of Speed here displays early and late racing models.

Also in Daytona: Baron Fun Frite's Castle, a funhouse with medieval theme – an amusement for children. Museum of Arts and Sciences has a collection of Cuban art. On the beach is the 176-ft sightseeing tower, the Space Needle.

Surfing championships are held at Daytona Beach during October and November, and a full range of watersports is available all year. Best tourist transportation is the 'Jolly Trolley' which travels along Atlantic and Volusia Avenues six days a week. Accommodations include the renovated century-old St. Regis Hotel.

De Land   D2

(pop. 13,600) A base for the outdoors enthusiast since there is easy access to several wilderness areas of interest. The town was founded in 1876 by Henry Deland who manufactured baking powder. Stetson University was founded here, in 1886, with the financial aid of John Stetson, manufacturer of the renowned hat. The university's theaters stage good winter season performances and the College State Basketball Tournament is held at Stetson's Edmunds Center in March. The annual De Land Artists Sidewalk Art Festival (March) attracts American artists from all over but there are also special events throughout the year.

Ponce de Leon came to within a few miles north of De Land and in honor of him the place was called **De Leon Springs**. Shaded by oak and cypress trees, the area has a great variety of bird life, Indian burial grounds, and recreational facilities. The springs themselves form a subterranean stream that pours out around 94,000 gallons of water a minute.

You can take a guided tour of the St. Johns River on a 17-ton sternwheeler which departs from near De Land. Or take the ferry to Hontoon Island, a 1650-acre island park with camping, fishing, boating, and picnicking facilities.

Fort Pierce   N8

(pop. 33,700) A citrus and vegetable center which took its name from the fort built here in 1838, a link in the chain of east coast defenses against Indian attacks. Its strategic position on the St. Lucie inlet gave easy communication by water to the north.

See the Fort Pierce Inlet Recreation Area with picnic, swimming, boating and fishing facilities in its 340 acres. **Pepper Park** includes St. Lucie Museum Recreation Area with sandy beach and treasure museum, and Jack Island Preserve. Seminole Indian artifacts are displayed in the St. Lucie County Historical Museum.

Melbourne   J6

(pop. 37,900) Midway down the central east coast, this town was named by an Australian for his native city. Sandy beaches, canals and a landlocked harbor

Kennedy Space Center

Merritt Island National Wildlife Reserve

tona Beach

tona International Speedway

Driftwood Inn, Vero Beach

give the town its special character, even though it has big city stores and shopping centers like Melbourne Square Mall with department stores and restaurants, and an industrial complex at Palm Bay. The city has its own zoo with over 300 animals and birds from around the world. Hotels include a Holiday Inn. **Melbourne Beach** is very isolated and favored by surfers.

New Smyrna Beach   D5

(pop. 10,580) This resort lies 14 miles south of Daytona and is much quieter. First settled by the Spanish in 1690, it became a producer of sugar and indigo when Mediterranean colonists moved in to establish plantations. See New Smyrna Sugar Mill Ruins, a 37-acre historic park with the remains of a sugar mill, a reminder of those plantation days. Also see Ponce de Leon Inlet Lighthouse, now a museum including a 175-ft lighthouse built in 1884, the keeper's cottage and artifacts of the sea.

Stuart   O8

(pop. 4820) A base for visiting the **Jonathan Dickinson State Park**, over 10,000 acres encompassing dense pine forests and parts of the wild Loxahatchee River. There are canoe trails along this river, nature trails and guided tours of the park and plenty of recreational facilities. Bikes and boats can also be rented in the park.

In Stuart itself see Elliot Museum, an art gallery, country store and unique auto collection. **Gilbert's Bar House of Refuge** is a museum on Hutchinson Island that displays nautical artifacts and relics

from shipwrecks. This is also a holding point for baby sea turtles.

Accommodations include a Holiday Inn and the Sandpiper Bay Resort. Small cruise boats leave from the latter for a tranquil trip up the north fork of the St. Lucie River, rich in wildlife. (The river was used for the boat chase scene in the James Bond movie *Moonraker*.)

Titusville   G5

(pop. 28,000) Located two miles from the Kennedy Space Center (pp. 18, 65), the main attraction, the town also offers water skiing, golf and fishing facilities. And it is a base for visiting Sebastian Inlet's **McLarty Museum** where slides and facility tours illustrate the salvage methods used to recover treasure from the Spanish fleet which sank off the area in 1715. Relaxation and recreation are the key to park activities near the northern end of the inlet. Catwalks under the inlet bridge are good for fishing and shrimping.

Vero Beach   M8

(pop. 11,908) A citrus area that extends across the Indian River. Skeletal remains found here along Van Valkenburg's Creek in 1916 were said to belong to the so-called Vero Beach Man, long believed to be prehistoric. Much speculation and controversy raged among scientists. Ultimately, the bones were proclaimed to be of Indian origin. The city's best-known landmark is the Driftwood Inn, built out of driftwood and old lumber in the 1930s by the late Waldo Sexton and furnished in eclectic fashion with cast-offs gathered from everywhere and anywhere.

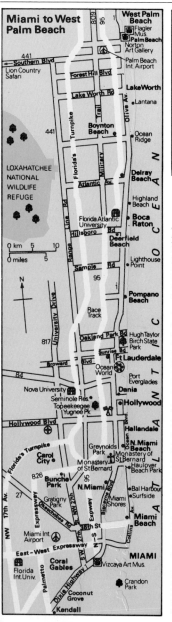

Miami to West Palm Beach

THE SOUTHEAST

The southeast encompasses the best-known parts of Florida, the most established resort areas and the most lavish properties. Miami may not be the state capital, but it is far more familiar and lively than Tallahassee. It is Florida's cultural center as far as theater and the arts are concerned – the nugget in the Gold Coast!

'Gold Coast' – America's Riviera – was a term coined for a unique string of resorts, marinas, racetracks, restaurants, shops, golf courses, yacht basins, hotels and villas and businesses of every description – all standing on what was once mangrove swamps: Miami Beach, Palm Beach, Fort Lauderdale, even its own Hollywood. It stretches for 70 miles from West Palm Beach to Miami.

The southeast, however, is more. A 200-mile stretch of coast extending from Jupiter to the Florida Keys, it embraces two national parks, ten state parks and some 150 campsites. A region no longer just for the wealthy. A region with a host of theme parks and amusements and a virtual paradise for the sportsman.

Sport here is more than a hobby, it is an industry. The southeast supports professional football and soccer, is spring training headquarters for five major league baseball teams, and hosts top men's and women's golf and tennis tournaments. Dog-racing, horse-racing and jai-alai seasons cover the whole year and quarterhorse and harness racing can be watched in their respective seasons.

Boating can, and does, mean anything from a houseboat to a sailboat to a cruise ship. Diving and sailboarding are a way of life. Nowhere else is the importance of the marine environment so visible as in this area where marine attractions and parks offer insight and prove invaluably educational.

In addition to its legendary beaches, the southeast has access to two other national treasures: the Everglades (p.53) and the aquamarine, reef-ridden waters of the Florida Keys (p.77). Its Intracoastal Waterway is a playground for all water-sports and yields effortless fishing. As they say, 'find a cluster of mangroves and drop a line'. It won't come up empty.

Fishing opportunities are legion. Many of the canals teem with bass. Lake Okee-chobee, 11,530 sq. mi. worth, also brims with bass and, in fall and winter, speckled perch. Offshore waters produce a volume of marlin, dolphin, bonita and sailfish. Boats can be chartered at any of the Gold Coast resorts for a half day, full day or longer. Nowhere is better for fishing than in the Keys where fish found nowhere else in North America may be caught. Best points to charter craft are Key Largo, Tavernier, Islamorada, Duck Key, Key Colony Beach, Marathon and Key West.

The Keys themselves – a chain of off-shore islands now linked completely by bridges to the mainland – are quite differ-ent from anywhere else in Florida. The pace here is slow and relaxed and you won't find concrete-box hotels or neon-lit nightlife. The Keys surround more than 100 remote isles, refuges for wildlife, in the Florida Bay.

When a developer is not picking a site in southeast Florida for a new hotel, someone will be sure to suggest a golf course or tennis complex. There are 17 golf courses in the vicinity of Miami alone and the region claims around 200 golf and tennis facilities in all.

Sport facilities are often associated with luxury resort hotels. The Boca Raton Hotel and Club is an example – almost a city in itself. Among the newer ones, Fort Lauderdale's Bonaventure Interconti-nental not only has two 18-hole golf courses, but is also a spa with exercise, hydrotherapy and diet programs tailored to individual guests' needs. Other top-bracket hotels include Miami Beach's all-suite Alexander. Each suite has a private terrace overlooking either the Atlantic Ocean or Indian Creek. Iced champagne and international newspapers are just some of the special features. Then there are the Hyatt Palm Beaches in West Palm Beach, the Hyatt Regency in downtown Miami, the Marriott in Fort Lauderdale, and The Pavillon, a world-class hotel located in Miami Center on the waterfront.

Southeast Florida's restaurants are unrivaled. Fresh local seafood and all types of ethnic dishes are readily available.

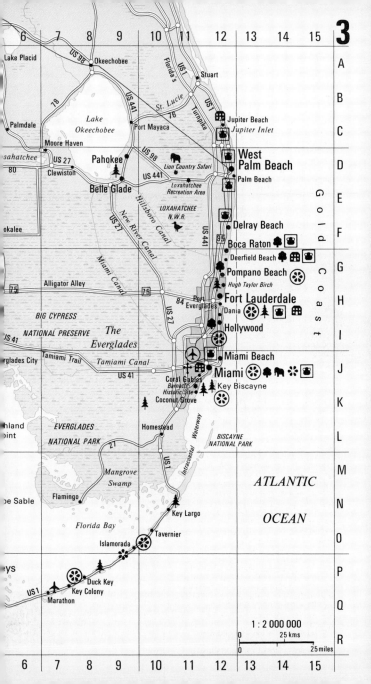

Some of the state's finest stores and boutiques and most interesting museums and galleries are located along the Gold Coast. Mansions such as Flagler's home, Whitehall, in the Palm Beach area and James Deering's Vizcaya, near Miami, are open to visitors.

As for history, don't miss a visit to one of the Indian Centers where Seminole and Miccosukee lifestyles can be seen. A Seminole visitor center and craft store is in operation at Hollywood and the Miccosukee tribe encourages visitors to their headquarters on the Tamiami Trail, 25 miles west of Miami.

Boca Raton   G12

(pop. 48,800) An attractive Gold Coast city, though its name means 'mouth of the rat'. The name came from the old Spanish maps which read *Boca Rattones* and was given because of the many sharp jagged rocks just below the surface at this point of the coast. The rocks and the domed thatched Indian huts near the beach led the Spanish to nickname the place 'rats' nests'.

Located about a half hour's drive from Fort Lauderdale, Boca Raton is Palm Beach County's second largest and most southerly city, covering 25 sq. mi. and seven miles of beach. In the 1920s town planners conceived it as a 'dream city'. At that time the El Camino Real (the main thoroughfare that runs to the sea) had a grand canal etched down the center and sightseers were borne along in electrified gondolas! The noted Florida architect, Addison Mizner, saw the city as an American Venice and the canal was decorated with ornamental landings and Venetian-style bridges.

The town was first laid out in 1897 after the arrival of the Florida East Coast Railroad. It was divided into ten-acre plots which were sold to apple planters. Up until Mizner's dream, it was a shipping point for winter fruit and vegetables.

Mizner created much of what is now the Boca Raton Hotel and Club. The 1925 original was a hotel named the Cloister Inn. Mizner took it over and transformed it into 'The Flossiest Hotel' around. Mizner's empire toppled with the collapse of the Florida land boom, though his style of architecture continues to survive. Since 1944 Boca Raton and its neighborhood have grown, sprouting condominiums, golf courses, yacht basins, holiday homes, flats, villas and shopping complexes.

It is a plush resort with lots to do. It has achieved recognition as a winter Polo Capital (Jan.–April) with Sunday games at the Royal Palm Polo Grounds. One of the most pleasant places to shop is the Royal

Palm Plaza which looks like a Spanish village with tropical walkways and blossom-hung boutiques. An evening out might include the Royal Palm Dinner Theater or dinner at any of countless specialty restaurants.

Outdoors there are two new city parks: Red Reef Park and Gumbo Nature Center. Inside, see the Singing Pines Historical Museum which depicts the history of the area and offers guided tours of Boca's oldest house.

Accommodations include a Sheraton and Holiday Inn.

Coconut Grove (see pp. 84–5)

Basically a suburb of Miami, best known for its Players State Theater which gives year-round performances, and its shopping facilities, particularly those at the Mayfair complex.

See also the **Barnacle Historic Site**, a five-acre park created round the pioneer home of Commodore Ralph Munroe who encouraged the construction near here of the first hotel in southern Florida, boosting the development of Coconut Grove (Wednesday guided tours).

Dania   H12

(pop. 9013) A resort one mile to the north of Miami. It used to be known as 'Antique Center of the South'. You'll still find a fabulous collection in a five-block area, though there are no bargains left. Dealers should visit the classic shops on US 1 and North East First Avenue. Alternative attraction is the two-mile palm-shaded beach with fishing facilities.

Deerfield Beach   G12

(pop. 29,700) Best known for Deerfield Island Park, an island in the Intracoastal Waterway. Once notorious as the island where Chicago gangster Al Capone hid out, it is now a fine spot for birdwatchers and accessible only by boat. Visit the **Loxahatchee Recreation Area**, a part of the Everglades where airboat rides are available and fishing and nature trails are a feature.

Of interest is the Old Schoolhouse, built in 1920 and since restored. It houses a 1915 piano and other 20s memorabilia. Pioneer House, built of Dade County heart pine in 1937, shows a typical example of a 'cracker' (pioneer) home.

Delray Beach   F12

(pop. 31,600) A resort not far from Miami. See Morikami Museum donated to the county by George Morikami, last survivor of the Yamato colony of Japanese pineapple farmers. Exhibits focus on Japanese folk arts and culture.

Morikami Museum, Delray Beach

Fort Lauderdale   H12

(pop. 146,000) A vacation city sometimes called the 'Venice of America', it has more than 165 miles of lagoons, canals and rivers. It is the county seat of Broward County, 25 miles north of Miami. It takes its name from Major William Lauderdale who gave his name to a fort built here in 1838 when he was commander of a Tennessee unit engaged in one of the Seminole Wars.

During Chester Arthur's administration, deeds to the shore went to private ownership and in 1893 a rich lawyer, Hugh Taylor Birch, bought three miles of coast. Today, the name of Hugh Taylor Birch is perpetuated in a 180-acre park which still includes Atlantic beachfront. A three-mile scenic railroad runs through it and there are outdoor sport facilities.

Neither the land boom collapse nor the 1926 hurricane stopped the tourists from coming to Fort Lauderdale. In its early days it was quite a 'Sin City' with an abundance of bars, gambling halls and brothels. Rum runners brought in so

much booze from Bimini in the Bahamas, that the city's nickname became Fort Liquordale. Among the more notorious rum runners was a man called Bill Macoy who satisfied the thirst of visitors with best-brand Scotch. Is is said that the drink he supplied was known as 'the real macoy'.

In the 1950s Fort Lauderdale entered a new phase with the influx of droves of college students who gave it a bright, vivacious image. And they still come each spring. With a superb climate and plenty of entertainment, hotels and eating places, it is a year-round resort. Shops, too, are tempting, especially on Las Olas Boulevard. It is one of the Gold Coast's most glamorous shopping streets, extending about a mile and a half from downtown. Another good shopping area is Sunrise Boulevard. Galt Ocean Mile and Plaza are good browsing areas for antiques and resort wear as is Sea Ranch Village Shopping Center at the east and northeast ends of Commercial Boulevard.

See Broward County Mini-Museum which features artifacts from the area's

Bahia Mar from the air

Fort Lauderdale beach

early days, and the Museum of Archeology where displays depict the life of Tequesta Indians who lived in the region before the Europeans arrived. Items include a 2000-year-old skeleton of a young Tequesta woman. Classical and modern works of art are on view at Fort Lauderdale Museum of the Arts. Anyone interested in steam trains should head for the Gold Coast Railroad Station and Museum where the southernmost operating standard-gauge steam train in the continental US is housed. Displays include the US Presidents' pullman.

Fort Lauderdale's **historic preservation district** is along New River at the Himmarshee Village (the name is a Seminole word for 'new river'). There are antique shops and restaurants here as well as the One-Room Schoolhouse and King-Cromartie House, furnished in period. The Discovery Center Museum lets visitors handle exhibits. Aquatic displays and photos plus other memorabilia are on display at the **Swimming Hall of Fame**. For marine fun, visit **Ocean World** which features dolphin and sea lion shows, shark tanks, etc. For evening family fun try Castle Park.

Of all the sports possible at this resort, boating has to come first. Facilities for chartering and sailing are excellent. The *Jungle Queen* paddlewheel sightseeing boat makes a three-hour cruise on the Intracoastal Waterway and New River, while the *Paddlewheel Queen* offers lunch or dinner cruises along the Intracoastal Waterway. Watersports and water theme parks are well to the forefront here. Waterslide Park on Eastern Park Boulevard is only two miles from the ocean and allows everyone a thrilling ride, regardless of age. **Atlantis, The Water Kingdom** has an 11-acre lake at its center. Located in the Greater Fort Lauderdale area, it boasts over a mile of water slides, water chutes and tube rides plus pools, waterski shows and hot-air balloon rides. The **Zoom Flume**, on US 441 and Sunrise Boulevard, has three separate tracks, totaling over 1000 ft of water slides. The Waterworks is yet another watery amusement.

One of the best ways to familiarize yourself with the city and its environs is to take the 18-mile **Voyager Train** tour past Port Everglades (departure point for major cruise ships), luxurious residential areas and Las Olas shopping areas.

Eating and entertainment are varied: rooms with a view, bars, clubs and lounges (more in ratio to its population than anywhere else in the US), cabaret, ethnic restaurants or Florida surf 'n' turf (lobster and steak). Most of the hotels, large and small, offer some kind of entertainment and/or music for dancing and almost all have more than one place to dine. Accommodations run the gamut from self-catering apartments or motels to luxurious Bahia Mar, Pier 66 and the Bonaventure Intercontinental. Waterfront dining is a plus factor at Bahia Cabana and Ocean Manor Resort Hotel. Guests at Bali Hai Polynesian Resort are treated to a sightseeing boat trip. Business oriented hotels include the Riverside Hotel and the Yankee Clipper Sheraton, or the new Marriott. Then there are the Windjammer Resort & Beach Club, the Holiday Inn and Harley Sunrise Inn – and literally countless others.

Hollywood   I12

(pop 115,000) A beach resort not far from Miami Beach or Fort Lauderdale. The Topeekeegee Yugnee Recreation Area is a pleasant lakeside park with bicycle trails and picnic pavilions; paddleboats and canoes can be rented. There are also tennis courts, soccer and baseball fields at a newer complex, the C.B. Smith Park, which offers similar amenities plus thrill rides.

Jupiter Beach   C12

(pop. 3136) An excellent spot for windsurfing in some of the world's best conditions for the sport. Its first international competition took place in 1983. See Jupiter Lighthouse Museum, a red-brick landmark perched on a bluff overlooking Jupiter Inlet. The lighthouse, still operational, contains local historic memorabilia. A view of the lighthouse and yacht-filled inlet may be had from the waterfront restaurants where seafood is top choice on menus, while the Burt Reynolds Dinner Theater is just down the street.

Facing the inlet is DuBois Home, the restored home of an early pioneer. There are Sunday tours of this house, built on Tequesta Indian burial ground. The Jonathan Dickinson State Park is not far from Jupiter and the *Loxahatchee Queen* sightseeing boat departs from here on river tours.

The Keys   Q3–Q6

The first explorers to sight the Florida Keys never stopped. Ponce de Leon called them Los Martires, The Martyrs, because they looked like suffering men. Pedro Menendez de Aviles also wended his way between the islands in his efforts to find a suitable channel for the Spanish fleet. But it was many years before the Indian inhabitants were actually disturbed.

Indian mounds dotting the keys suggest that the Arawak and Caribee tribes may have been the first to live on the islands, but they were driven out by the fierce Calusa, expert seafarers and fishermen. The Calusa are known to have been based in at least two villages, Cuchiyago and Guarugunve, where they stashed treasure taken from wrecked or pirated vessels.

The Spanish called them *cayos* (small islands) and 'key' is merely an English modification. The way of life between Key Largo and Key West goes at a slower pace than anywhere else in Florida. And many a Miamian nips to the Keys for a weekend of fishing, boating or simple relaxation. These days you can drive all the way on US 1, thanks to brilliant engineering feats with bridges.

From the southern tip of mainland Florida, the islands form a 150-mile arc reaching into the Gulf of Mexico. Many of them are little more than a few hundred yards wide, blanketed with mangroves and punctuated by Caribbean pine and silver palmetto. An offshore coral reef (the reason for so many wrecks and pirates in bygone days) surrounds the islands.

Part of the reef can be seen in close-up at the **John Pennekamp State Park**, located at *Key Largo*, the first and longest of the keys. The park is heaven for scuba and snorkeling enthusiasts. Within its 150 square miles of Atlantic Ocean, there are hundreds of species of tropical fish and a multitude of different corals. Best overall view is from a glass-bottom boat, though there are scuba diving tours of the reef, too. All necessary equipment can be rented from the park's headquarters. Closer to shore canoe trails wind through the mangrove swamp and there is a roped-off swimming beach and camping facilities.

Sands Key, Elliott Key and *Old Rhodes Key* in the Biscayne Waterway are focal points for the annual Columbus Day Regatta in October when 300 sailboats head into Biscayne Bay, many overnighting on Elliott Key. Between Elliott Key and Old Rhodes Key is a tiny island known as Black Caesar's Rock, once a pirate stronghold. It is said that Black Caesar was a negro slave who escaped and pirated ships single-handed until he became Blackbeard's trusty aide. Legend also claims he kept a harem of women and maintained a prison camp near Elliott Key.

The section of the archipelago between Key Largo and Long Key is known as the **Upper Keys** and is particularly easy to reach from Miami. Tavernier, associate of the pirate Jean Lafitte, gave his name to *Tavernier Key*, as it was one of his favorite hiding places. Today from here ornithologists can go on tours to the Florida Bay Rookeries. To the south, *Plantation*

Key took its name from the fact that pineapples and bananas once flourished here.

Islamorada is a famous and popular sport fishing center on *Upper Matecumbe Key*. The key itself is said to have taken its name from an Indian corruption of the Spanish *mata hombre* 'kill man', which was also the meaning of Cuchiyago, the Indian name for the island. At Islamorada the many coral reefs in the surrounding shallow water offer scuba and skin divers an interesting time. Of particular note are The Underwater Coral Gardens and the wreck of a Spanish galleon. Theater of the Sea, near Islamorada, is an outdoor sea aquarium.

Long Key is another stop for snorkelers. Dive shops arrange individual or group trips to the nearby reefs to hunt for crawfish. And in Layton you'll find the Zane Grey Creek and Sea World Shark Institute. Long Key State Park has its own camping facilities and nature trail.

The section between Long Key and the Seven Mile Bridge is known as the **Middle Keys**. Minuscule *Grassy Key* is said to have been named for an early settler, not the vegetation. In the early part of this century a pile of gold was dug up on the key, so no doubt many pirates once buried their treasure here. Today, look in at Flipper's Sea School and Porpoise Training Center.

The next key of any importance is *Marathon*, once known well to such pirates as Morgan, Lafitte and Teach. Today it is a developed tourist center with its own airport, convention center and 18-hole golf course. A paradise for fishermen and boaters, it has retained enough of its fishing village ambience to give it charm.

Between the Seven Mile Bridge and Key West is the area known as the **Lower Keys**, the largest of which is *Big Pine Key* with acres of thick silver palmetto, Caribbean pine and cacti. With luck you might spot one of the tiny key deer or the rare white heron. The Bahia Honda State Recreation Area offers rental of scuba and skin diving equipment and has picnic facilities, campsites and coral-free swimming.

Of all the keys, *Key West* is the most famous, most popular and boasts the most accommodations. It is known that, in 1700, the Calusa Indians, who held the tip of the peninsula, were driven out by British Indian allies. Key West was incorporated as a city in 1828 and its population was soon increased by fugitives from the Indian massacres in the Upper Keys. Transplanted British loyalists came here via the Bahamas and Bermuda. Yankee seafarers sought refuge here. And in 1869

Shrimp boats, Key West

Audubon's House, Key West

Sunset in Key West (Background)

Marathon Key

Cubans started coming here to establish cigar factories. Island-born Key Westers, descendants of this mixture, call themselves 'Conchs' (pronounced *conks*), the name of the edible mollusk noted for its admirable shell, so be prepared to hear and see the word around a lot.

A much-loved haunt in the past of smugglers and rum runners, Key West still houses and attracts a diverse set of people. Dope smuggling still goes on here. There is a very large resident 'gay' community. And no one hurries. 'Funky' would probably sum up Key West better than 'laid back' though, after the Sunday afternoon poolside tea dances at gay-oriented La Terraza de Marti, quite a few people are laid out!

Though all the development is taking place in the new section of Key West, it is the old quarter with Duval Street as its main artery which has the character: 19th-century sea captains' houses with widow walks (now often guest houses), masses of bougainvillea, frequent spectacles at Mallory Square, and a leisurely tempo.

Accommodations There is a large Marriott hotel in Key West but probably the best hotel is Pier House on the water in Old Town, at the foot of Duval Street. The rooms have a view of the harbor, the Gulf, the pool or the gardens. Originally an 1890 conch house, the Pier House is a spirited but elegant place to stay.

There are lots of guest houses with anything from 4 to 17 rooms. Some have small swimming pools on the property, some include continental breakfasts in their rates. A few, like La Terraza de Marti, have restaurants, others have kitchen facilities. Many are run by 'gay' management though the clientele need not necessarily be exclusively gay.

One of the better (and larger) establishments is Island City House, built in the 1880s as the home for a rich Charleston merchant family who turned it into a hotel in anticipation of the arrival of the railroad in 1912. All 18 one- and two-bedroom apartments have kitchens and there is a pool and jacuzzi. Hurricane Alley near the hub of Old Town activity has two-bedroom cottages with kitchens for rent and a sun/pool area. Among the more economical guest houses Merlinn is rather pleasant. The proprietors ensure a homey social atmosphere and lay on a complimentary cocktail and hors d'oeuvres at Happy Hour time.

If in doubt about the right kind of accommodation for you, contact Key West Discovery (530 Simonton St, Key West, tel: 305 294 7713), a free accommodation service that advises and makes bookings.

Eating and Drinking Conch (the food) turns up in a variety of ways on many menus, most usually as a chowder or fritters, and can be very tasty. The other item to look out for is key lime pie. Made with real key lime juice, the authentic dessert is a creamy (not lime) color. If it is green, food coloring has been added.

Duval Street is a good place to start. Bagatelle here, in a lovely old conch house, specializes in Caribbean cuisine, but there is a number of eating places along this thoroughfare from breakfast diners to sidewalk cafes and good restaurants. Away from Duval Street, well-known and well-recommended restaurants are Louie's Backyard and Harbour Lights.

There are plenty of places to drink, often in courtyard settings – try Michael's which also has a disco. Most bars offer discounted Happy Hour prices. There are several discos, many predominantly 'gay', a theater and a couple of cinemas. While Key West is the liveliest of the keys, action is not round the clock, so expect the sidewalk to roll up reasonably early.

Duval Street, by the way, is the best shopping street as far as boutiques go, but prices tend to be high as Key West is considered trendy. A fun handmade fabric alligator, for example, might run to $300.

What to See Don't miss the sunset from Mallory Pier, it's a must. Everyone raves about the colors of Key West sunsets. And the going down of the sun brings out the magicians, musicians, jugglers and dancers who create their own spectacle.

Ernest Hemingway's House, a Spanish colonial stone house on Whitehead Street, is another attraction. Hemingway loved Key West, lived with his second wife here and used the town's locale in many of his short stories and novels such as *To Have and Have Not*. While here he also wrote *For Whom the Bell Tolls* and *Green Hills of Africa*.

The appeal is that the furniture and memorabilia were Hemingway's own rather than, as the guide says, 'old'. The photographs remind one how handsome the writer was as a young man – not surprising that he was married four times. (Granddaughters, Margot and Meriel are daughters of the son of his first marriage.) The little touches are the most interesting: the Hemingways kept cats, 72 of them, and the numerous cats around today are descendants. The second Mrs Hemingway considerably lightened her Nobel-prize-winning husband's wallet when she spent $14,000 on a swimming pool – but then it was the first in Key West and had to be hewn by hand out of coral rock.

John James Audubon, the ornithologist, also stayed for a while in Key West.

He visited in 1832 aboard the revenue cutter *Marion* and spent time making sketches of birds and plants he discovered ashore. The **Audubon House** is also on Whitehead Street.

President Harry Truman had a winter home here: the little white house just beyond the western end of Southard Street, which was remodeled for him after his first visit to Key West in 1946. It was here in 1948 that he held the Key West conference of joint chiefs-of-staff to work out plans for the unification of the armed services.

The **Lighthouse Museum**, on Whitehead Street, is operated by the Key West Art & Historical Society and contains several military exhibits, including a Japanese submarine captured at Pearl Harbor. On Duval Street, **Oldest House Museum** is an 1829 sea captain's house. The construction, with the famous 'landlubber's tilt' and ship's hatch in the roof, shows the influence of early shipbuilding. Inside is a furnished dolls' house and models of ships.

For the children, Key West Aquarium at Mallory Square shows off sharks and other marine life, while dolphins perform at Flipper's Sea School on Roosevelt Boulevard.

The best way to see Old Town is by **Conch Train Tour**. It's really a little tram that chugs round town while all major sights are pointed out, including the Spanish galleon in the harbor – one more reminder of the island's pirate days. You will also see the old conch houses belonging to shipwreck salvagers and the Key's shrimp fleet. As an all-weather alternative, Old Town Trolleys also take you round town the easy way.

Sightseeing by water is a further possibility. Key West Sightseeing Boat makes several daily cruises, including a sunset cruise with live music. The schooner *Western Union* takes you back to the days of the sailing ship. And *Fireball* Glass-Bottom Sightseeing Boat introduces visitors to the wonders of the sea surrounding them.

Special time of year is between January and April when **Old Island Days** takes place – a series of exciting events designed to interest the visitor, they also help to preserve Key West architecture, history and customs. During this time, many houses in private hands are open to the public for day or evening tours. Events might include art festivals, food festivals concentrating on Key West specialties, craft shows, readings from Tennessee Williams (another island devotee), or parties sponsored by different organizations or individuals.

Key West, like the other keys, is renowned for its fishing. More than 600 varieties of edible fish are to be found in its surrounding waters. Sport fishermen can find tarpon, dolphin, amberjack, etc. Anglers can try their hand from the docks, piers and bridges. Half- and full-day deep-sea fishing excursions can be easily arranged and there is also a seaplane service to the Dry Tortugas, some 68 miles west of Key West.

Key West has its own airport and Alamo rent-a-car offers free pick up and delivery with unlimited free mileage from its base at the Key Wester Inn.

Miami   J12

History In the 17th century Spanish maps marked what we know to be Miami as 'Ayami' or 'Mayami' – derived perhaps from the Indian words *maiha* (meaning very large) and *mih* (it is so). Early settlers, following the Indians, certainly formed a hamlet here on the edge of a large subtropical wilderness. Fort Dallas was established at the mouth of the Miami River to control the Seminoles, but it was abandoned several years later leaving only a few of its garrison to eke out a living.

Though there were many pioneers eager to see Miami grow, until Julia Tuttle came along there was no large-scale interest. Daughter of a Florida state legislator, Mrs Tuttle frequently visited Miami and bought land in the 1870s. After the death of her father and husband, she moved permanently to Miami in 1890. Knowing that the only way for Miami to grow was via a railroad link with the rest of the state, she had long tried to persuade the tycoon Henry Flagler to extend his Florida East Coast Railroad from Palm Beach to Miami. With no luck. The Big Freeze of 1894/5, which destroyed Florida's citrus and vegetable crops as far south as Palm Beach, changed his mind. And when Julia Tuttle sent him frost-free orange blossoms from Biscayne Bay to prove her point, he came south to look and to negotiate.

Mrs Tuttle and the neighboring Brickells offered him land in return for extending the railroad, making civic improvements and building a hotel. Streets were cleared, a waterworks and electric plant installed, and, in 1896, the rail link was completed bringing in building materials and people. That year, Miami became a city and the first luxury hotel, the million-dollar Royal Palm complete with swimming pool, was opened in January of 1897.

When the Spanish-American War broke out profiteers and troops poured in. The summer of 1898 was a prosperous

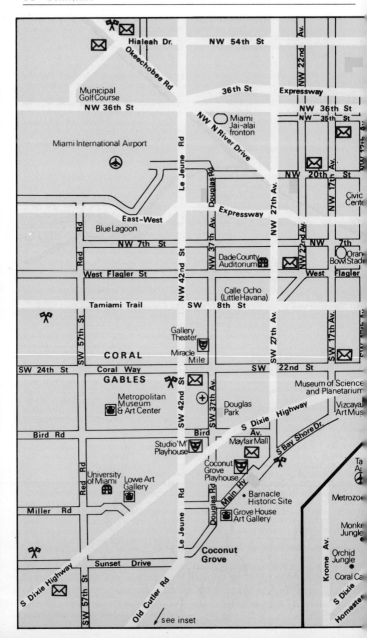

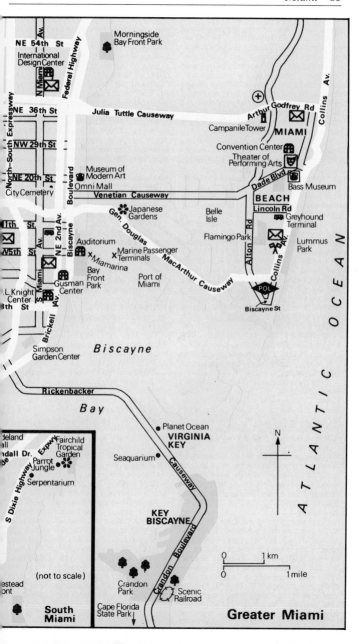

NE 54th St
International Design Center
Federal Highway
N Miami Av.

Morningside Bay Front Park

NE 36th St
Julia Tuttle Causeway
Arthur Godfrey Rd
Collins Av.

Campanile Tower
MIAMI

North-South Expressway
NW 29th St

Convention Center
Theater of Performing Arts

NE 20th St
City Cemetery
Boulevard
Museum of Modern Art
Omni Mall

Venetian Causeway
Dade Blvd
Bass Museum

BEACH
Lincoln Rd

11th St
Gen. Douglas
Japanese Gardens
Belle Isle
Greyhound Terminal

5th St
NE 2nd Av.
Biscayne
Auditorium
Marine Passenger Terminals
Flamingo Park
Alton Rd
Lummus Park

Miamarina
MacArthur Causeway
Collins

Miami Av.
Gusman Center
Bay Front Park
Port of Miami

.L. Knight Center
8th St
Brickell
POL
Biscayne St

Simpson Garden Center

Biscayne

Rickenbacker

Bay

A T L A N T I C   O C E A N

deland all
Kendall Dr.
S Dixie Highway
Expwy
Fairchild Tropical Garden
Parrot Jungle
Serpentarium

Planet Ocean
VIRGINIA KEY

Seaquarium
Causeway

KEY BISCAYNE

N

(not to scale)

Crandon Boulevard

estead ont

South Miami

Crandon Park
Cape Florida State Park
Scenic Railroad

0   1 km
0   1 mile

Greater Miami

one. Farmers shipped tomatoes at $1 a crate. Fifty-foot lots on Flagler Street (then 12th St) sold for $1000. The following year, what had been used as a parade ground for the troops found itself a golf course and electricity and telephones came to Miami. Though a yellow fever epidemic, fire and a hurricane in 1906 all caused damage, Miami didn't give up. An inland waterway was made between Miami and St. Augustine, and the dredging of Government Cut made it possible for Miami's harbor to accommodate large ships.

To the early tourists Miami Beach, an island between Biscayne Bay and the Atlantic, was a mosquito-infested swamp, though they sometimes went there to picnic or bathe. New Jersey horticulturist, John Collins, gets much of the credit for the island's development. At first he tried to grow fruit and dredged the canal from Indian Creek to Biscayne Bay to provide water transport, but when his fruit-growing venture failed he organized a residential community and began construction of a bridge across the Bay. In 1913 the two-mile, wooden Collins Bridge linked Miami Beach with Miami.

The land boom raced ahead. Street naming was standardized. By the 1920s the south Florida boom was in its heyday. Everyone wanted a piece of the action. Poet, George Merrick, schemed to build 'a place where castles in Spain are made real' – Coral Gables. The city was born in 1925, not quite to Merrick's plan, though there are still elegant gates around the Gables and streets there often bear Italian or Spanish names.

That year was the crest of Miami's wave. Hialeah was born and Hialeah Horse Track opened with 16,000 patrons. Miami's skyline continued to grow. Daily air service between New York and Miami was inaugurated. 481 hotels and apartments were built. And land was going for thousands of dollars. Just one year later the boom ended with the 1926 hurricane. Winds were measured at 138 miles an hour before the instruments blew away. Homes were leveled, boats were sunk, property damage reached the billion dollar mark. Suddenly, land which had sold for $60,000 was selling for $600.

But Miami recovered. New buildings were constructed, Biscayne Boulevard dedicated, and, in 1928, Pan Am set up a small airfield on the present site of the international airport. Despite another horrific hurricane in the 30s, expansion carried on and a second land boom took place after the end of World War II when several new causeways were built across Biscayne Bay, including the $6 million Rickenbacker Causeway to Key Biscayne.

To counteract a fall in tourism in recent years, Greater Miami has been busy. The four-acre City of Miami/University of Miami James L. Knight International Center, with the 615-room Hyatt Regency as part of the complex, opened in 1982. Behind it lies the $1 million Miami River Walkway. New hotels are numerous and Miami International Airport has made significant improvements. At the Port of Miami a quarter-billion-dollar development plan is in progress and the billion dollar rapid transit system, Metrorail, began service in 1984 on a ten-mile route from the Dadeland shopping area in the suburbs to the downtown cultural center. A monorail system within central Miami's business district is due to open in 1985. Aventura is a new shopping mall, downtown's largest. Constant additions are made at Metrozoo. And Miami Beach has a new beachfront park and promenade, new sport facilities, and there has been renovation and revitalization of the shopping districts and the art deco area.

What the visitor must remember is that Greater Miami (Metropolitan Dade County) actually comprises 27 municipalities plus some unincorporated areas, sprawling across more than 2000 square miles.

Where to Stay The choice of where to stay is obviously considerable so opt for *area* first. Do you want to stay downtown, at The Beach, in villagey Coconut Grove? Then choose type: a motel, a prestigious hotel, a business hotel or self-catering. And only then ask about price.

Downtown: the 19-story, 615-room Hyatt Regency overlooks Biscayne Bay and its location on the appropriate highway gives easy access to the airport. (Downtown streets can clog with traffic.) It offers full-service restaurants, lounges and a swimming pool and is suited to business or holiday guests. The nearby Riverparc, on the other hand, is specially designed for business people. Each of the 135 suites is furnished with a computer terminal and all the necessities of a private office in a luxury setting. A private club lounge, fitness center and pool are added benefits.

Major downtown thoroughfare is Biscayne Boulevard, the location of several hotels including the Omni International, part of an admirable complex with shops, restaurants, cinemas and an amusement area. On the roof there are tennis courts, a pool and a children's playground. Within the complex there's a 24-hour child care center and nursery school and the amusement area includes a carousel. Also on the Boulevard are the Mardi Gras Motel, the Marine Park and a Howard Johnson's. A plush Miami addition is the Pavillon which is part of the $1.1 billion Miami Center complex. Key features here are its all-oak lounge, its Italian marble bathrooms and fully-stocked bars in every room. There are 636 rooms, seven restaurants and lounges, a pool and tennis and racquet courts. A new 615-room Marriott also overlooks Biscayne Bay in downtown Miami.

In chic *Coconut Grove*, a chic new hotel, the Grand Bay, (the Italian grand hotel chain CIGA's first in America) is the choice of the well-heeled. Its distinct pyramid-shaped building houses 200 rooms and suites which are furnished with antiques, feature fully-stocked bars and have a TV in the bathroom. Full gourmet dinners can be ordered from a 24-hour room-service menu as an alternative to using the restaurants. Concierge and other personal services plus a chauffeur-driven limousine to take you to business or shopping appointments help to add a touch of old Europe to this part of America. The hotel also houses Regine's Nightclub.

In *Miami Beach* the Fontainebleau Hilton is one of the most complete resort hotels along Collins Avenue, but a whole string of hotels of all kinds lines this oceanfront boulevard. Old names like the Eden Roc and Beau Rivage have spent money on renovation while the first new hotel to be built since 1967, the 300-room Meridien, will rise as part of the 'Two Worlds' complex at Collins Avenue and 47th Street. The Alexander is a Seacoast Towers Apartment Hotel with one- and two-bedroom accommodations, each with living and dining rooms, kitchen and private terrace. Facilities include the first-class Dominique's restaurant.

Now that the emphasis is placed on preservation rather than demolition, a nice hotel note in Miami Beach are the **Art Deco Hotels** which boomed in the years of the Great Depression. Two good examples have been restored: the Cardozo and the Carlyle Hotels standing together on Ocean Drive, looking across Lummus Park. Though both are listed on the National Register, they do offer modern comforts such as air conditioning, color TV and bathrooms. Fruit and flowers welcome guests on arrival and there is a concierge to help with any needs.

The Cardozo has 70 rooms and was built in 1939. Before World War II, it was one of Miami Beach's most fashionable hotels and, in the 50s, it was the setting for Frank Sinatra's movie, *Hole in the Head*. Its Cafe Cardozo today features a light tropical menu and contemporary jazz. The 76-room Carlyle Hotel reopened in 1982 as a classic example of art deco revival. Its grill room specializes in

seafood and steaks and there is live piano music in the background. Within the vicinity are some 800 small hotels, shops and residences that make up the Art Deco District and, just a few blocks away, the Flamingo Park Tennis Center, the Bass Museum, the Theater of the Performing Arts, the Miami Beach Convention Center and, a landmark, Joe's Stone Crab Restaurant.

A cluster of hotels/motels are also to be found across the causeway on Key Biscayne itself. Key Biscayne Hotel & Villas is among the most upper-crust establishments, but you will also find a Sheraton Royal, Sonesta Beach Hotel & Tennis Club and Silver Sands Motel on Ocean Drive.

Eating Out In addition to the multitude of fast food outlets, there are many ethnic quarters where the food is excellent and the atmosphere evocative of the home country. In the Little Havana district of downtown Miami, for example, there is a good sprinkling of Cuban restaurants as well as Spanish and Mexican influences. The main thoroughfare is Calle Ocho (SW 8th Street). De Malaga, a comfortable Spanish tavern, is on this street as is El Bodegon Castilla and Vizcaya. Cuban sandwiches are good at El Pub and Versailles, also on SW 8th Street. 'Carnaval Miami' takes place around Calle Ocho each March when the entire Hispanic community throws a block party for everyone. Street dancing, parades, fireworks and, of course, lots of Spanish specialties are the order of the day.

In addition to the Latin influence, Miami has numerous other ethnic restaurants: Hungarian, Belgian, Indian, Vietnamese, Jamaican, Korean, Argentinian, Brazilian, Creole are all represented here. And for those who fancy a picnic, but don't want to get too far out of downtown, Watson Island (midway between downtown and The Beach) is the place.

Each community (Miami Beach, Coral Gables, Coconut Grove, etc.) offers its own eating and drinking places. As with all cities, names tend to change, but one famous, long-established, seafood restaurant is Joe's Stone Crab, located on Biscayne Street, Miami Beach, which has won many dining awards. Stone crabs are in season from mid-October to mid-May.

Entertainment If you take into account all the communities, there is a nightlife for everyone, from discos, showy revues to concerts and other cultural performances. Most nightclubs are located in downtown Miami, in the large hotels of Miami Beach and in Coconut Grove and Little Havana. When a big name tops the bill expect the prices to reflect accordingly.

Miamarina

SUNWARD II

Along Key Biscayne

Cruise ships in the port of Miami (Background)

Venetian pool, Coral Gables

Windsurfing

Crandon Park, Key Biscayne

Big room dinner shows are usually to be found at Miami Beach, and the Fontainebleau Hilton and Sheraton Bal Harbour both specialize in this type of nightclub show. One of the newest and most fashionable discotheques is Regine's in the Grand Bay, Coconut Grove. Polynesian food and show are offered by Wong-Kai at Omni International. A Latin-flavored revue is featured by Copacabana in Little Havana and a mixed crowd opts for the Spanish music and dance revue at Flamenco Supper Club on NE 79th Street or the Las Vegas-style show at Les Violins Supper Club on Biscayne Boulevard.

Entertainment, other than the big shows, runs the gamut from quiet piano music to pop or jazz bands (Gaslight Club or Bogey's, both on Collins Avenue, Miami Beach).

For a more cultural evening out, try the following which stage musical, theatrical or dance performances at varying times of the year:

Dade County Auditorium (varied entertainment), 2901 W. Flagler St, Miami. Tel: 545 3395.

Greater Miami Opera Assn. (Jan.–Apr.)

Miami Beach Theater of the Performing Arts, 1200 Coral Way, Miami. Tel: 854 1643.

Gusman Cultural Center (varied entertainment), 174 E. Flagler St, Miami. Tel: 358 3338.

International Cultural Exchange (international performers), Dade County Auditorium, 2901 W. Flagler St. Tel: 642 8000.

Key Biscayne Concert Series, Rickenbacker Causeway, Virginia Key. Tel: 361 7441.

Miami Beach Theater of the Performing Arts (varied entertainment), 1700 Washington Ave. Tel: 673 8300.

Miami Convention Center (varied activities), 400 SE 2nd Ave, Miami. Tel: 372 0929.

P.A.C.E. (free concerts in area parks). For information call 856 1966.

Players State Theater, Coconut Grove Playhouse, 3500 Main Highway. Tel: 442 4000.

Ring Theater (Collegiate), University of Miami Campus. Tel: 284 3355.

University of Miami Music Dept. (various). Tel: 284 2433.

Sport A host of sports both spectator and participant are available to the visitor to Miami. (See Enjoy Yourself.)

Shopping In every location, there is a good choice of shopping in boutiques, major department stores and traffic-free malls. Each community has its own selection. Main department stores include Bloomingdale's, Burdine's, J.C. Penney,

Jordan Marsh, Lord & Taylor, Neiman-Marcus, Saks Fifth Avenue. The following are a few suggested shopping areas:

Aventura Mall (one of the newer ones which includes a branch of Macy's, high fashion and budget), 19501 Biscayne Blvd, Miami.

Bal Harbour Shops (exclusive, prettily designed mall with stores like Gucci), Collins Ave and 97th St, Miami Beach.

Cutler Ridge Mall (major department stores and boutiques), Caribbean Boulevard and US 1, Miami.

Dadeland Mall (one of the largest malls), 7535 Kendall Dr. and US 1, Miami.

Lincoln Road Mall (a tram travels the eight blocks of shops, many of which are boutiques), 76th St, between Washington and Alton Roads, Miami Beach.

Little Havana (from Cuban coffee and sandwiches to cigars or furniture), SW 8th St, Miami.

Mayfair-in-the-Grove (exclusive boutiques like Valentino), 3390 Mary St, Coconut Grove.

Omni Mall (two-level shopping plaza of mixed stores), Biscayne Boulevard at 16th St, Miami.

163rd St Shopping Center (moderately priced shops), North Miami Beach.

The Falls (one of the newer centers), US 1 and SW 136th St, Miami.

What to See Downtown, the newest achievement is the **Metro-Dade Cultural Center**, at 101 W. Flagler St, housing a library complex, the Historical Museum of Southern Florida, and the Center for the Fine Arts. The Mediterranean-style complex covers a city block and is built round a plaza 14 ft above Flagler St. Entrance to the arts center is by covered walkway off the central plaza. At first floor level, there is a theater, gift shop, lobby and 7000 sq. ft of exhibition space. On the second floor, there is another 10,000 sq. ft of exhibition space. In addition to the main galleries, the center has a 3000 sq. ft sculpture court, an 1800 sq. ft auditorium and a bookstore. Exhibits change from time to time but 'The Great Horse' by Raymond Duchamp-Villon will remain permanently on show in the sculpture garden.

The Historical Museum made its move from Vizcaya to the northeast corner of the courtyard. Original documents in the Research Center, which also houses original letters and documents of Miami's founders, Henry Flagler, Carl Fisher and George Merrick, may be used by the public.

Even if you're not buying or eating, enjoy a browse along **Calle Ocho**, on SW 8th St, between SW 11th Ave and SW 19th Ave, to see the sidewalk flower sellers, outdoor murals and domino playing.

An unusual point of interest is the **Miami City Cemetery** at NE 2nd Ave and NE 18th St. It is the burial site of such well-known names as Julia Tuttle and Dr James Jackson, for whom Jackson Memorial Hospital was named.

Since it opened in 1981, Miami's **Metrozoo** has become the city's major attraction. It is cageless. The animals live on moat-surrounded islands – tigers without bars if you like. The second phase in 1983 included a free-flight aviary and an African section. Touring the zoo may be done on foot, by tram or by monorail. It is located at 12400 SW 152nd St, just west of the Florida Turnpike exit.

Most of the Miami attractions like the Metrozoo are mentioned in Young Florida (p.19) as they are geared to families but, in addition, see **Coral Castle**, 28655 S. Federal Hwy, tel: 248 6344, a romantic if out-of-place structure comprising 30 tons of rock hoisted into place by a Latvian immigrant for love of a woman who jilted him the day before their wedding. Open daily 9am–5pm. The Spanish **Monastery of St. Bernard**, 16711 W. Dixie Hwy, tel: 945 1462, was originally built in Spain in 1141. Millionaire publisher, William Randolph Hearst, bought, dismantled and shipped it here in 1925. It contains priceless art works and antiques, and is open 10am–4pm Mon.–Sat.; 12–5pm, Sun. **Castle Park** on Griffin Rd, exit off Interstate 95 – 1999 SW 33 Pl., is for the kids, with an 18-hole miniature golf course, bumper boats, water flume ride, go-karts, etc. Open 10am–12am Mon.–Fri., to 1am on weekends.

Coral Gables is most famous for its 'Miracle Mile' shops. It is green and pretty with some lovely homes, and it was here that the University of Miami was founded. All kinds of campus activities keep the area lively and there's good theater and several art galleries in the vicinity. Some major business companies have moved here adding a commercial zing and a few mini skyscrapers.

The community with the most character is **Coconut Grove**, still called 'a village'. Wealth is here. You can see it in elegant homes hidden by bougainvillea and the banyan, oak and poinciana trees arching over the streets. You can see it in the Rolls-Royces that take the Grove for granted and the sleek yachts in the marina. Americans say it's Europeanized because of its sidewalk art shows, its little bistros, its cafes serving croissants and espresso.

It loses its charm somewhat in the rain, but pottering around makes for discoveries: small galleries and boutiques tucked away into alleys, or a sight that doesn't fit into the rest of Miami. Commodore Plaza is one of the main browsing areas. Kennedy Park's Vita Course is for workouts. There are bike paths, a private sculpture garden just over the bridge at Grove Isle, and historic Barnacle House built before Miami was a city. There are hotels, restaurants and nightclubs and a celebrated theater here. On weekends the Coconut Grove Tram operates to show visitors village attractions. Not far away, Deering's famous winter home, **Vizcaya**, stands majestically in its estate, where Sound and Light performances are given on weekend evenings mid-May to mid-September. The house was started in 1914 and as many as 1000 craftspeople worked on it during the years following, creating a Renaissance villa said to be among the finest in America.

Key Biscayne, crossed via Rickenbacker Causeway from Miami (for a toll), is a place unto itself. It is an island with luxury homes and hotels. It has fine restaurants, a few shops and acres of parkland and beach. Only when the causeway was constructed in 1947 did city dwellers realize the full potential of this idyllic weekend retreat. World spotlight shone on the key when President Nixon chose it for one of his holiday White Houses.

The Miami **beach** scene rundown is as follows, from south to north:

Homestead Bayfront Park, N. Canal Dr. Tel: 247 1543. Picnicking, boating and ballgames are more popular here than actual swimming.

Matheson Hammock Park, 9610 Old Cutler Rd. Tel: 666 6979. Good for children to bathe from. There are lifeguards and a large saltwater pool away from the shoreline. Sailing and swimming classes are given, there are play and picnic areas, trails and places to fish from.

Bill Baggs Cape Florida State Park (on Key Biscayne). Tel: 361 5811. A two-mile stretch of well-kept sandy beach, shaded picnic area and a restored lighthouse which probably warrants the park admission charge.

Crandon Park Beach (on Key Biscayne). Tel: 361 5421. 960 acres of park include a beach patrolled by lifeguards, picnic/grill areas, a miniature golf course, amusement park, miniature railroad and outdoor roller skating rink. There are showers, concession stands and a special pathway for the handicapped to reach the beach.

Hobie Beach is the name given to the stretch of sand each side of the highway, just past the tollbooth on Rickenbacker Causeway. Mostly for windsurfers and sailboats.

Polo at West Palm Beach

Virginia Beach (Virginia Key). Open only on weekends but with soft sand and lots of privacy.

Pier Park (southernmost point of Miami Beach) is best for surfing. Free fishing off Municipal Park Pier.

Lummus Park (Miami Beach), between 6th and 14th Sts, offers a smooth sandy beach, clear water and a few shady palm trees.

Thirtyfifth St Beach (Miami Beach) is close to the Fontainebleau Hilton. A good place for shell collecting.

Fortysixth St Beach (Miami Beach). Favorite gathering spot for guests of the big hotels. Catamaran, windsurfing and boat rentals are all available here.

Seventysecond & Seventyfourth St Beach (Miami Beach). Good swimming attracts a mixed crowd.

North Shore Open Space Park (Miami Beach) 79th–87th Sts. A shady area with a boardwalk, vita course and concert offerings.

Bal Harbour (just north of Surfside Beach). Sea grapes and palm trees provide the scenery and the shade. Good for shell hunting. Also a vita course.

Haulover Beach Park, A1A north of Bal Harbour. Tel: 947 3525. Named because people hauled their boats over the beach to get to the water. Popular with the young crowd. Barbecue area; a small charge for fishing off the pier; good for surfing.

Miami has a bounty of museums (see p.44).

Palm Beach   D12

(pop. 505,000) An elite Riviera-style beach resort adored by the hedonists, it boasts some of the country's most beautiful villas and claims to have more Rolls-Royces on its streets than London.

Neither the Spanish nor the British in their time made anything of this delightful spot. It was during the Civil War that a draft-dodger settled here and built the first house. By 1873, four families resided here. Captain Elisha Newton Dimick is usually credited with founding Palm Beach when he arrived in 1876, but its reputation as a resort is probably due to a Spanish shipwreck of 1878. The cargo of coconuts was washed ashore and early settlers, planting them on their own land, transformed what had been an uninspiring sandy key into a place of beauty. In 1880, the settlers named their town Palm City but, discovering that the state already had a town of that name (near Stuart), they rechristened it Palm Beach. The pioneer hotel was Henry Flagler's Royal Poinciana, soon patronized by Philadelphia society. With such a stamp of approval, more luxury hotels, wealthy estates and exclusive clubs were quickly built.

If Palm Beach looks a little like Italy's Portofino, it is due to the architect Addison Mizner who arrived in poor health in 1918, prepared to die. Instead he met and became friends with Paris Singer (son of the inventor of the sewing machine) and, backed by his wealth, decided to put his energy into creating rather than dying. He designed the celebrated Everglades Club which attracted socialites like the Vanderbilts. Then he built opulent homes for them. There were no bricklayers when he arrived in Palm Beach and, to get the irregular tiles he wanted, Mizner had to create a whole new industry to produce Mediterranean-style, bright-glazed tileware.

Pompano Beach

This is the resort with a name for names. Gucci and Cartier labels litter the stores along Worth Avenue, one of America's most famous shopping streets at the heart of Palm Beach. British royalty has played polo at the Palm Beach Polo and Country Club in West Palm Beach. And The Breakers hotel is a deluxe seaside palace (once the private palace of the Flagler family).

The classic way to tour the Palm Beaches is an elegant whisk round in a Rolls-Royce or Bentley, and one of the options is an evening out with dinner at the Poinciana Club plus a seat for the performance at the Royal Poinciana Playhouse. A less gold-plated way to discover the area is by Pierrebus which starts from Riviera Beach. Highlights of the area are included in several different tours.

See the Hibel Museum of Art honoring the painter Edna Hibel, and the Society of the Four Arts, a museum complex with gallery, library and garden. Not to be missed is the **Henry Morrison Flagler Museum** at Whitehall, the fabled multimillion-dollar white marble mansion which the railroad pioneer, Flagler, built for his third bride. After the Flaglers died, most of the original furnishings were removed from the mansion which was sold as a hotel in 1925. The property was reacquired and is now restored to reflect its former brilliance. The Rambler, Flagler's private railroad car, is a permanent exhibit on the estate's grounds. Younger tourists may be more interested in the Palm Beach County **Planetarium and Science Museum** in West Palm Beach, or **Lion Country Safari**, about 15 miles to the west of West Palm Beach.

The Palm Beaches are noted for super-duper hotels. Among the newer ones are the Royce and the Hyatt Palm Beaches, both in West Palm Beach.

Pompano Beach   G12

(pop. 52,100) A neighboring resort of Fort Lauderdale, it is the winter base for the Goodyear Blimp; a visitor center gives the history of the flying machine. Shops are concentrated in Fashion Square at 23rd Street, an airy, landscaped mall decorated with sculpture. Ocean Side Center, a few yards from the beach and hotels, is also recommended for shopping. Florida's first mountain waterslide, Waterboggan, is located a mile north of Fashion Square, its design inspired by alpine tobogganing. Three courses have over 1000 ft of raceways. In Trade Winds Park you can fish the lake, swim, hike or horseback ride.

A wide choice of hotels, restaurants and nightclubs gives Pompano Beach its popular appeal. As an added attraction, the *Hidden Harbor* showboat offers lunch or dinner cruises along the Intracoastal Waterway.

Singer Island

This is the spot where the Gulf Stream waters come closest to land, keeping the temperature constant: cooler in summer but warmer in winter than most other areas of Florida. Its biggest attraction is the public beach which is wider than any other along the Gold Coast. It is only a 15-minute drive north from Palm Beach but can offer lower-priced accommodations. For shops, nightspots and restaurants look to Ocean Mall. All types of watersports are available. Vacation apartments are plentiful and both Sheraton and Hilton have properties here.

Royal Palm Avenue, West Palm Beach

CENTRAL FLORIDA

As its name suggests, central Florida is the state's heartland. In the sprawl of land and water between Ocala National Forest and Lake Okeechobee there is both variety and adventure. Central Florida is Disney World and EPCOT, plus innumerable other fun and fantasy parks and attractions, several of which opened before World War II. Yet it is also fruit and vegetable country, lake country and cattle country.

Cattle came before citrus, and though, when farmers learned that orchards could be more profitable, much of the ranching moved south, central Florida still supports a major beef and dairy industry. For the visitor the main interest is the area's rodeos. In the Kissimmee area the state's largest rodeo, the Silver Spurs, is held and in the Arcadia area, the oldest, the All-Florida Championship Rodeo.

Citrus groves offer a treat to delight the senses – fragrance during blossoming seasons and a sparkling taste whenever you buy fruit from roadside stands or pick your own from the trees: oranges plus tangelos, satsumas, tangerines, grapefruit and many others.

Often central Florida is referred to as 'Lake Country'. Look at a map and you'll soon see why. Amid the rolling hill country lie literally thousands of lakes – Lakeland embraces 13, Winter Haven 100. Lake Wales sits in a lush setting. Two of the state's largest streams, the Peace and Kissimmee rivers, flow almost its entire length.

With so many lakes, anglers are in for a good time. Any required tackle and equipment may be rented at most lakes and rivers where there are also camps providing accommodation. Watersports for the whole family are possible on lake and riverside. No coastline, but still limitless opportunities for swimming, snorkeling, scuba diving and boating for pleasure. The central area includes the Ocala National Forest which has two popular recreational areas within it. Both have camping, picnicking and fishing facilities around bubbling springs, but there are less-developed parts of the forest for those who prefer to rough it.

Ocala is the place for horse farms (p.16). Its natural attributes are similar to Kentucky's famous Bluegrass country. Florida has 475 registered thoroughbred horse farms, many of which can be toured by parties interested in the breeding and training of champions. As far as betting goes, central Florida has harness racing,

greyhound racing and jai-alai in their respective seasons.

Florida is a web of walking trails and the central region is no exception. One of the newest trails to become part of the National Trails System is 15 miles on the Avon Park Air Force Range, not too far from Sebring and Lake Wales. It starts and ends at campgrounds, passing Fort Arbuckle, a Seminole War landmark, and old sheep and cattle camps along the way.

Interspersed among the lakes and forests are over 100 challenging 18-hole golf courses, often with tennis courts attached. Some resorts own more than one – the Grenelefe Golf and Tennis Resort boasts three golf courses. If you happen to be under 18, there is professional instruction on the six-hole, par 23, Wee Links Golf Course at Walt Disney World Resort.

Though the region's early attractions brought a steady stream of tourists, it was Disney's decision, in the mid-1960s, to site Disney World in the vicinity of Orlando that sparked off the development and facilities you see here today. It brought Orlando's airport to international standard, and it brought numerous hotels and motels, better transport facilities, more restaurants (there are 3000 eating places catering to all tastes and pockets), new shops like Kissimmee's Mill Creek, and a vibrant nightlife.

The opening of the $900 million EPCOT Center, in 1982, did even more. The Orlando Marriott Inn is the area's largest full-service resort and Sheraton World is Sheraton's largest franchise. Buena Vista Palace, located in Walt Disney World Village, has amenities which include a tropical free-form pool, health spa and marina. Next to the Village, Vistana Vacation Villas is the first timeshare operation, with an expansive hotel/villas tennis complex. Villa features include jacuzzis and kitchens equipped

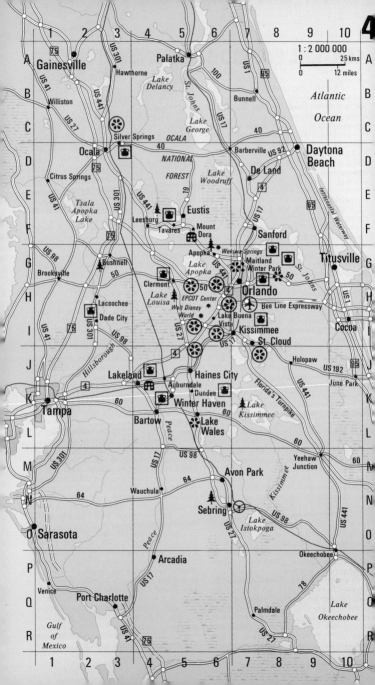

with microwave ovens. Properties along US 192 have grown at record speed to provide visitors with a wide choice of accommodations in all styles. The renovation at Silver Lake Lodge in Ocala has turned it into one of central region's best motels. And upgrading goes on apace, while new buildings continue to appear.

Besides Disney World, there are water theme parks, alligator farms, wax works, zoos and gardens. Shows at theme parks (including Disney World and EPCOT) range from dixieland bands to top-name entertainers, from discos to country and western.

Apopka   G6
(pop. 4045) Eight miles northwest of Orlando, Apopka is called 'Houseplant Capital of the World', but what makes it a vacation base is Wekiwa Springs, a park of more than 6000 acres where you can picnic, swim, scuba, boat or take a nature trail. A canoe trail starts here and extends for 26 miles to the St. Johns River.

Auburndale   J5
(pop. 5386) East of Lakeland, Auburndale and vicinity host innumerable events throughout the year. There are tours of the Jacquin Distillery to see how liquor is produced.

Clermont   H5
(pop. 3661) In the heart of citrus country, close to all of central Florida's theme parks, it is most notable for its 200-ft **Citrus Tower**, highest point in the area. From the top you can see more than 17 million citrus trees. Also see the House of Presidents Wax Museum which contains lifesize models of US presidents in period settings. Seven miles south west is **Lake Louisa**, a park covering almost 2000 acres with facilities for swimming, fishing and picnicking.

Kissimmee   I7
(pop. 7119) Major vacation base for central Florida, popular for its proximity to a number of attractions. Two alligator farms, for example, are within an easy drive: Alligatorland Safari Zoo and Gatorland Zoo. The latter has a nusery for 1000 one-year-old alligators plus many full-grown specimens and there is a miniature train to transport those who don't care to take to the boardwalks. Kissimmee also has the Hawaiian Slip Water Slide which provides 1000 ft of water flumes.

On the museum side, Indian World Museum houses thousands of Indian relics and memorabilia. And an unusual one, Tupperware Museum & International Headquarters, displays historic food containers, demonstrates Tupperware products, and shows the manufacturing process. Also in Kissimmee see the Monument of the States, a landmark comprised of stones from 48 states and 23 countries.

Lakeland   K4
(pop. 48,900) A resort in the heart of citrus country, though Lakeland also has a noted phosphate industry. Of special interest is Florida Southern College which was designed by Frank Lloyd Wright. The Polk Public Museum houses art and artifacts.

Lake Wales   L6
(pop. 8240) A resort on Lake Kissimmee surrounded by a park (once ranchland) with all the lakeside recreations you'd expect: fishing, boating, nature trails. At the top of Iron Mountain is **Bok Tower Gardens**, a peaceful retreat built in the early 1900s by Dutch immigrant, Edward Bok, for whom the sanctuary was named. The tower houses a 53-bell carillon which gives daily recitals. At Citrus World they tell you all about the product and hand out a free sample of orange juice.

Mount Dora   F5
(pop. 4543) A quaint country town with a New England atmosphere. Draped over hillsides, the town is dotted with citrus trees and interlaced with lakes. The 'Mile of Beauty' tourist route leads past wealthy homes but a landmark is Donnelly Mansion, a piece of Victorian 'gingerbread' built in 1893. Even the business district has a distinct 'other era' air about it with its colonial street lamps and brick planters.

Orlando   H7
(pop. 113,900) The hub of central Florida with a $300 million international airport. Orlando has grown in little more than 50 years from a small-time trading post on a cattle range to an impressive city whose boulevards and parkways are handsomely landscaped and lined with oak and camphor trees.

The city was settled after the Seminole Wars (1835). The site was chosen close to Fort Gatlin, established in 1837, for its proximity to good water and habitable highlands. Since the garrison offered protection, a number of settlers headed toward Orlando, named around 1850. Why the name? It could have been to honor the hero in Shakespeare's *As You Like It*, but it was more likely chosen to commemorate Orlando Reeves, a runner between Mellonville and Fort Gatlin, who was slain by Indians on the site of the town.

Very much a citrus center, Orlando's first commerical grove was planted on 100 acres in the 1860s. Vegetables, particu-

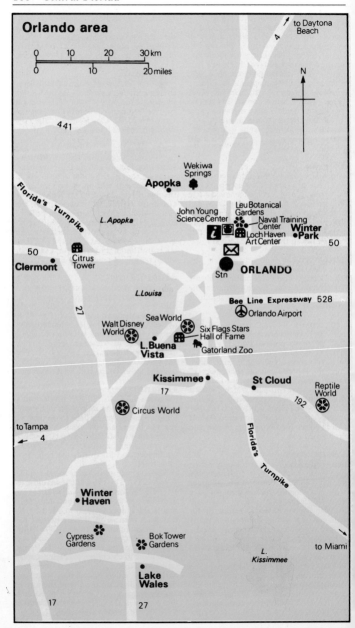

Orlando area

0 10 20 30 km
0 10 20 miles

N

to Daytona Beach

4

441

Wekiwa Springs

Apopka

L. Apopka

Florida's Turnpike

John Young Science Center

Leu Botanical Gardens

Naval Training Center

Loch Haven Art Center

Winter Park

50

50

Clermont

Citrus Tower

27

L. Louisa

ORLANDO

Stn

Bee Line Expressway 528

Orlando Airport

Walt Disney World

Sea World

Six Flags Stars Hall of Fame

L. Buena Vista

Gatorland Zoo

Kissimmee

17

St Cloud

192

Reptile World

to Tampa

4

Circus World

Florida's Turnpike

Winter Haven

Cypress Gardens

Bok Tower Gardens

L. Kissimmee

to Miami

Lake Wales

17

27

Disney World Fun Fair

Sea World, Orlando

Racing at Sebring

larly tomatoes, grow in abundance in this area – you'll see them on roadside stands. Orlando is the trading and distribution center for the region's extensive farming industry, but highway construction and a hotel boom in the 70s made it more of a tourist base for the attractions like Disney World in and around it.

There are (besides Disney World p.23) Sea World, Stars Hall of Fame, Wet 'n' Wild, Circus World, nearby Cypress Gardens (all featured in Young Florida). There is Florida Festival where Florida foods and festivals are featured; Mystery Fun House with 15 entertainment areas located under one roof; the John Young Science Center with scientific exhibits and a planetarium. History is on show at the Loch Haven Art Center and the Leu Botanical Gardens display tropical and subtropical flowers. Every Friday a 50-state salute is given at graduation ceremonies at the Orlando Naval Training Center.

A host of places to stay, in all price brackets, includes Hiltons, a Marriott, Sheratons and Orlando also has a variety of restaurants and nightspots. One established complex is Church Street Station where there are four themed eating places with entertainment, including Rosie O'Grady's Goodtime Emporium.

St. Cloud   I7
(pop. 5041) One of the country's largest working ranches is located here. The Mormon Church owns the 310,000 acres, split into 16 mini-ranches, plus 2400 acres of citrus. Reptile World Serpentarium is

also in St. Cloud; demonstration of venom extraction is one of the features.

Sebring   N6
(pop. 7223) A town synonymous with Grand Prix racing. The Florida 12-hour Grand Prix of endurance was instigated in 1952 and has been held annually in March ever since. Celebrated drivers come here to compete for cash prizes and to gain World Championship points.

Silver Springs   C3
(pop. 900) A natural attraction in the Ocala area, the springs discharge 500 million gallons of water a day. In the recreational area visitors may take a jungle cruise or a glass-bottom boat ride, visit the deer park or reptile institute, and look at a collection of vintage cars or prehistoric canoes. Not far away are two theme parks: Six Gun Territory and Wild Waters.

Winter Park   G7
(pop. 21,700) An attractive residential town, just north of Orlando, with tree-shaded streets and scenic lakes. Florida's oldest college, Rollins, was founded here in 1885. Its gardens and estate are best viewed on one of the guided boat tours. Also see the beautiful Knowles Memorial Chapel Garden, the baroque Annie Russell Theater, and the Cornell Fine Art Center housing three galleries of American and European art. The Morse Gallery of Art holds the world's biggest private collection of Tiffany glass and the Beal Maltbie Shell Museum has two million shells!

THE WEST COAST

The west coast is a place of contrasts, man-made and natural, modern and wild. It has a 28-mile stretch of shimmering white sand beaches: the Pinellas Suncoast communities extending from St. Petersburg to Tarpon Springs. There is an international airport at Tampa and the area affords easy access to the fun parks of central Florida. And it is less expensive to stay and to eat here than on the southeast coast.

It was a holiday find years back. Henry Plant extended his railroad and steamship routes into Tampa in the 1880s and opened the Tampa Bay Hotel in 1891. The area became a fashionable winter resort of the wealthy. Today, you don't have to be wealthy to enjoy the Gulf of Mexico's shoreline, uncrowded and uncluttered. Be a beachcomber, go shelling, fish, waterski or sail.

The west coast has islands – Sanibel and Captiva or Marco – where latterday Robinson Crusoes can luxuriate. South of Marco Island you can explore by boat the wilderness of Ten Thousand Islands, a cluster of mangrove islands surrounded by waters rich in the silvery game fish, tarpon. Points of entry are Marco, Goodland, Everglades City and Chokoloskee.

A premier tarpon fishing area (mid-May until Aug. is the best season), the west's bridges and piers can be used for hooking trout or snook. Offshore fishing is just as popular. Party boats and charter craft are available at Tarpon Springs, Dunedin, Clearwater, St. Petersburg Beach, Tampa, Bradenton, Sarasota, Venice and Englewood. And noted rivers for freshwater fishing include the Crystal, Homosassa, Hillsborough, Manatee, Braden and Peace.

The region encompasses twelve state recreational areas and Withlacoochee State Forest where camping, canoeing and hiking are year-round activities. Nature lovers never have to travel far. One of the highlights of the area is Corkscrew Swamp Sanctuary, near Bonita Springs, maintained by the National Audubon Society. In the wild sections of the west, threatened species like the American alligator, Florida panther and the bald eagle have found refuge.

Golf and tennis are well catered for in over 100 plush courses and racquet clubs. Resort complexes such as Saddlebrook and Innisbrook emphasize superb greens. Island golfing might mean staying at the Dunes Golf and Tennis Club on Sanibel, which has an 18-hole course. Villa-style accommodations are popular in the area. Boca Grande Club on Gasparilla Island

has club villas, tennis villas and marina village units. On Marco Island, Eagle's Nest Resort resembles something plucked from the South Seas. Gulf-front villas feature paddle fans, whirlpool baths and complete kitchens. Seawatch On-the-Beach, at Fort Myers Beach, offers villas suited to lengthy stays. The intimate Tortuga Beach Club on Sanibel Island is yet another villa accommodation. Dude ranches, sailing adventures, overnight canoe trips, cruises from St. Petersburg are all part of a west-coast vacation.

There is a leisurely atmosphere in this region and a certain elegance to cities such as Fort Myers, Bradenton and Naples. On the cultural side there may be surprises. The Ringling Museum complex, in Sarasota, includes a major art collection and an 18th-century theater which was dismantled in Italy and shipped to Florida by John Ringling in 1950. St. Petersburg's Salvador Dali Museum is another unexpected house of art.

Family fun isn't forgotten. One of the state's major attractions, Tampa's Busch Gardens/Dark Continent, is in this region. As with other theme parks, this one is constantly expanding. There is also long-standing Weeki Wachee with its 'mermaid' shows. Fantasy Isle in Fort Myers is a newer children's delight. And at Jungle Larry's African Safari, the public can view the training methods used on tigers and bears in TV and the movies.

Natural springs, gardens and opulent homes should be on the sightseer's itinerary. Thomas Edison chose Fort Myers as his winter home, initially living in one of the country's first prefabs while he worked on his inventions, and then moving to a riverfront house still filled today with his own furnishings and light bulbs. Gamble Mansion near Bradenton, once focal point of a large sugar plantation, is also noteworthy.

Clearwater   F3

(pop. 72,300) The seat of Pinellas County, occupying a high coastal position, it is one of eight beach communities comprising the Pinellas Suncoast. Nicknamed 'The Sparkling City' for its sparkling Gulf waters and subtropical vegetation, Clearwater is a family vacation center where watersports are given a high priority. Sailing, water skiing, windsurfing, snorkeling and boating are all possible. Events taking place here include the Kahlua Cup International Yacht races.

Fish from Pier 60 which stretches 1100 ft into the Gulf. Try surf-casting at Clearwater Pass, try shore casting from the Memorial Causeway or rent a charter boat from Clearwater Marina. The white sand beach itself, two miles of it, lies on an island between the harbor and the Gulf; from downtown it is reached via the Memorial Causeway.

Several sightseeing boats depart from Clearwater's marina: daytime, sunset or dinner/dance. One afternoon excursion is on board a 'buccaneer' boat with the crew in full pirate regalia; the price includes soft drinks and rum.

Sport is not restricted to water. The Philadelphia Phillies use the resort for training. This major league baseball team is based at the Jack Russell Stadium. More than a dozen good golf courses are in the area and there's lots of tennis. The annual Fun 'n' Sun Festival lasts a week (in March), with tournaments and competitions in a host of sports.

Of note is the recently opened Ruth Eckerd Hall in the Richard B. Baumgardner Center for the Performing Arts, second only to Bayfront Center in St. Petersburg. The 2000-seat theater will hold an extensive schedule of activities. See also Yesterday's Air Force & Museum on Fairchild Drive where restored aircraft and aviation artifacts are displayed.

Most of the local restaurants specialize in fresh seafood. Entertainment varies from rock to steel bands. And accommodations include the Holiday Inn Surfside plus the Belleview Biltmore Hotel.

Dunedin   F3

(pop. 25,900) A residential beachside town adjoining Clearwater, Dunedin is a primarily Scottish community founded by Scottish settlers in 1870. That heritage is visible in the architecture, the street names and in the festivities. No lack of bagpipes here.

Before the railroad came through this area, Dunedin was one of the chief Gulf ports between Cedar Key and Key West, shipping fruit and vegetables by schooner. Historically registered buildings in Dun-

edin are Andrews Memorial Chapel and J.O. Douglas House. The Dunedin Railroad Historical Museum on Main Street was originally the railroad station for the Orange Belt Railroad system dating from 1889. Memorabilia from the town's Scottish past can be viewed here.

The Scottish heritage is also celebrated in a number of annual events such as the March Highland Games Festival. There is a kirk organ series between October and May and the Dunedin Bagpipe and Drum Corps holds free community concerts.

An attraction for Dunedin visitors is the morning ferry from the Municipal Marina across to lovely **Caladesi Island**, accessible only by boat. More than two miles of unspoiled white sand beaches are to be found here and the state park is a refuge for wading birds. There are food and picnic facilities plus a children's playground.

Or take the car across the causeway to **Honeymoon Island**, another state park of tropical beauty with its own recreation area. Patient anglers can bring in good-sized snook here.

Fort Myers   K6

(pop. 37,500) Now a museum, Thomas Edison's winter home for 50 years is located at 2350 McGregor Boulevard, Fort Myers. Originally, his home was the country's first prefab where he experimented with the goldenrod weed as a source of rubber and also worked on other inventions. Then he moved to the riverfront house you see today, furnished as it was, with his light bulbs, of course.

Southwest of town is the area's first major theme park, **Fantasy Isles**, where storybook characters may tower as high as 40 ft. Accommodations include villas for long stays at Fort Myers Beach in the Seawatch On-the-Beach complex.

Holiday Isles   F3

The name given to six beach communities, though they've recently become known also as the Gulf Beaches. They are: Indian Shores, Indian Rocks Beach, Belleair Beach, North Redington Beach, Redington Shores and Redington Beach. Between them they have ten miles of sands and, at Indian Rocks Beach, the longest fishing pier in Florida. Each beach is different but along any of them you can bike, jog, go shelling, sunbathe or swim.

Boating as elsewhere along the Pinellas Coast is ideal. The temperature and the water are just right. Novice sailors can rent boats and get instruction at any of the Holiday Isle beaches. Rent a powerboat, if you wish, and go waterskiing on the Intracoastal Waterway.

Indian Rocks Pier, closely followed by

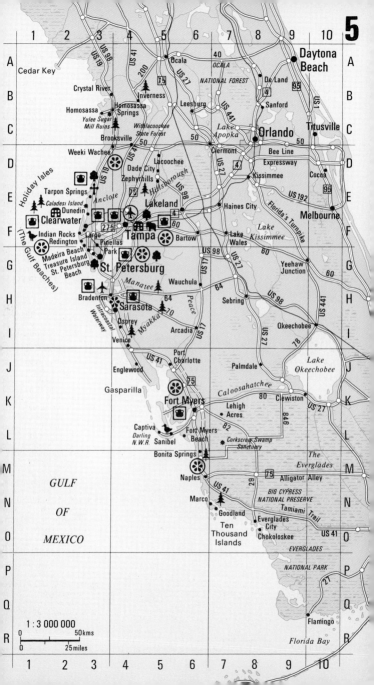

Sanibel Island: one of the best shelling beaches in Florida

Redington Long Pier, are much favored by fisherfolk. The catch might include kingfish, grouper, snook or barracuda.

Two of the Hinellas' main attractions are in the Holiday Isles. The **Suncoast Seabird Sanctuary**, 18328 Gulf Boulevard, Indian Shores, is open daily during daylight hours welcoming visitors for free. It is a refuge for some 500 land and sea birds who have been injured or crippled. You might well expect to see here brown pelicans, cormorants, bald eagles and white herons. **Tiki Gardens**, at 19601 Gulf Boulevard, is a Polynesian adventure trail designed to simulate a South Seas Island with tropical gardens, shops and a restaurant with an oriental touch.

Madeira Beach   F3

(pop. 4177) In the center of the Pinellas Suncoast, this resort has one of the best fishing inlets in the state at Johns Pass – big-game or casual, the fishing's famous. Charter boats at the municipal marina set out for deep-sea catches; rental boats are also available for inland fishing on Boca Ciega Bay.

Madeira's beach, north of Johns Pass, is about 2½ miles long with powder-fine sand. Johns Pass Village is an atmospheric collection of boutiques, galleries and restaurants in the style of a traditional fishing village.

Marco Island   N7

A delightful offshore island retreat with its own hotels, restaurants and shops. Near the western border of the Everglades, the Eagle's Nest Resort boasts two spas and gulf-front villas; Marriott's Marco Beach Resort, in the southwest, has its own shopping arcade. The way to get around is by 'Marco Moo Trolley'.

St. Petersburg   G3

(pop. 241,500) This city, most cosmopolitan of the communities along this stretch of coast, occupies the southern tip of the Pinellas peninsula. Few examples remain of the town's early Spanish architecture, the pseudo-Spanish style which became so fashionable in the days of the land boom is more predominant now.

Good weather and a healthy climate made it a winter haven, especially for the elderly, but the number of man-made attractions and its own festivals and sporting events have all given it youthful oomph.

Narvaez, the Spanish explorer, landed somewhere along the Boca Ciega waterfront in 1528, but the first recorded white settler didn't arrive here until 1843. He was John C. Williams of Detroit, founder of St. Petersburg. He bought land in 1876

that was to become the nucleus of today's city. He soon gave up attempts to farm and turned his hand to town planning in the course of which he made a deal with Piotr Alexeitch Dementieff, an exiled Russian nobleman who changed his name to Peter Demens. Popular history has it that the two men tossed a coin to name the new town. Demens won and christened it St. Petersburg after his own home town.

Wherever you stay in St. Petersburg, you won't be far from a beach. Bay beaches downtown are fine to swim or snorkel from. The wide, white sand Gulf beaches are about a half hour away. They call the city a sailing capital and boating opportunities are numerous. Prestigious racing events and regattas take place annually here and rentals of all types of boats are easily available. Charter boats head for big game fish from Pinellas Point; other boats leave from any of the four gulf-front fishing piers. Municipal piers and bridges also provide walkways for fishermen.

In season, from Jan. to May, there's greyhound racing. Baseball fans can see the New York Mets and St. Louis Cardinals, both of whom use the town as a base for spring training, while the Tampa Bay Rowdies soccer team has an indoor season at the Bayfront Center. With seven golf courses and 75 lighted public tennis courts, there's little excuse for not playing.

The **Haas Museum**, on 2nd Avenue South, includes the Lowe House, built in 1850, and the Grace Turner House. Free afternoon guided tours are given at the **Museum of Fine Arts** on Beach Drive North, where there are antiques and art works. The world's largest collection of works by the Spanish Surrealist, Salvador Dali, is displayed at the **Salvador Dali Museum** on 3rd Street South. Photographs and memorabilia from the past are on show at the **St. Petersburg Historical Museum** on 2nd Avenue NE.

Don't miss seeing the HMS *Bounty*, a wooden replica of the 18th-century ship on which Fletcher Christian led a mutiny against Captain William Bligh in 1789. This reproduction was built for the 1960 movie, *Mutiny on the Bounty*, and is berthed in the Vinoy Basin. For nature lovers, Boyd Hill Nature Trail covers 216 acres. Boardwalks and six trails wind through this city park which is home to native wildlife. In Sunken Gardens, on 4th Street North, more than 5000 tropical flowers and plants are on show. The menagerie of birds and animals includes an enormous walk-through aviary. A biblical wax exhibit, restaurant and gift shop are also part of the complex.

When it comes to dining and entertainment, St. Petersburg has the most to offer

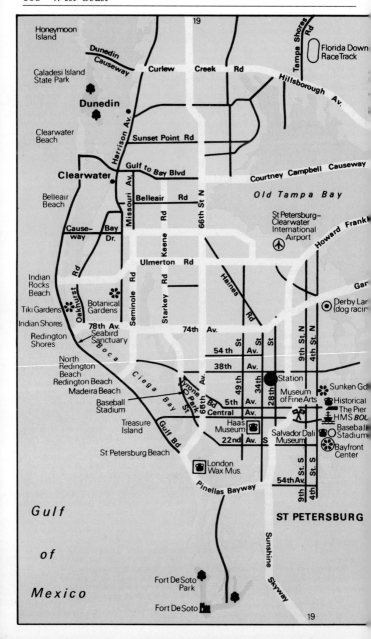

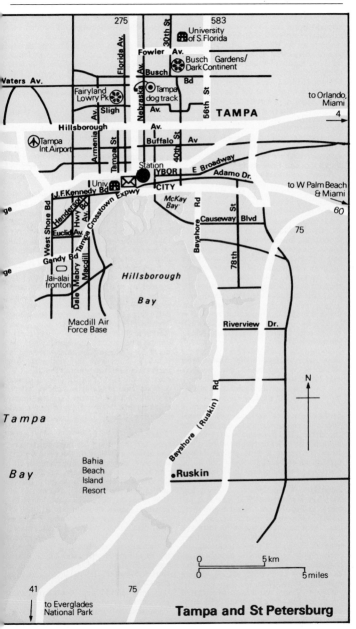

Tampa and St Petersburg

along this coast. The range includes big-name shows at the Bayfront Center, dinner theater at the Golden Apple, classical concerts by the Florida Gulf Coast Symphony, Broadway shows in one of the theaters, nightclubs and intimate dance lounges. One place everyone stops at is the Million Dollar Pier, a cluster of restaurants and lounges, and the Isle of Nations shops, all on St. Petersburg's waterfront.

Of St. Petersburg's 31 recreational parks and 30 scenic parks, Fort DeSoto, at the southern tip of the Pinellas, is of note. The fort was built during the Spanish-American War and now watches over 884 acres covering six islands, seven miles of waterfront and three miles of beach.

Accommodations include a Hilton and the Bayfront Concourse Hotel.

St. Pete Beach   G3
(pop. 8024) Seven and a half miles of silver sands run the length of this resort which is an island connected to the mainland. Waterfront hotels, beach bars and snack bars at the public beaches at Pass-a-Grille and Upham Park provide all necessary facilities. At several local marinas you can rent waterskis, catamarans, jet skis or windsurfers. Fishing options include the grass flats in Boca Ciega Bay or big-game fishing offshore in rented party boats. Recommended local spot to drop a line is the Pass-a-Grille seawall and jetty. Of some nine public tennis courts, eight are lit for night play.

Should the weather take a turn for the worse, take the family to the **London Wax Museum** on Gulf Boulevard. There are over 100 figures, some by Louis Tussaud. (Or there are the St. Petersburg attractions just up the road.)

Restaurants suit every taste, with a predominance of seafood and oriental dishes. Accommodations range from the expensive down to simple beach cottages. Nightlife includes discos, piano bars, jazz clubs (including a good one at Pass-a-Grille), cabaret lounges and a club at the north end featuring nightly singalongs.

Sanibel/Captiva   L5
Two island resorts reached via the causeway from Fort Myers. Once there, the best form of transport is bike or moped. Both islands are particularly noted for the number and variety of shells found on their beaches. Some 300 types, including the multi-colored calico shells, have been recorded here. The beaches themselves are excellent for swimming, sailing, fishing and other watersports.

Captiva Island was a favorite retreat of President Theodore Roosevelt, who often came deep-sea fishing here. One of the rewards of the visit is the **Darling National Wildlife Refuge**, on Sanibel Island, best experienced by canoe. Sanibel accommodations include Tortuga Beach Club with health club, tennis courts and gulf-front villas, and the Casa Ybel Resort. The Dunes Golf & Tennis Club claims the only 18-hole course on either island and also has a heated pool.

Sarasota   H4
(pop. 173,000) A compact city 53 miles south of Tampa. The coast round here is indented with bays and tiny inlets, and a chain of offshore islands offers the sunbather superb white sands. The city may well have taken its name from a corruption of the Spanish expression *sarao sota* 'place of dancing'.

Home to many retired naval and army men, Sarasota also has a resident winter colony of professional baseball players. Fishing is the number one sport – from the beach, out in a boat, or in Myakka River Park, a 28,857-acre wildlife preserve with all the associated leisure facilities: nature trails, camping, boating, etc.

See Bellm's Cars and Music of Yesterday with its fascinating collection of hurdy gurdies, nickelodeons and old cars. Marie Selby Botanical Gardens, once a private estate, was opened to the public in 1975. Main Sarasota attraction is the **Ringling Museum Complex**. The late John Ringling chose the city as winter headquarters for his circus in 1929 and built his home here. The fortune amassed from his circus business went into the estate, his magnificent art museum and the development of the islands in the bay. Also see Sarasota Bonsai Gardens with its collection of 2000 trees, and the Sarasota Jungle Gardens with 5000 species of palms and flowering shrubs.

Tampa   F4
(pop. 269,000) Florida's third largest city and major gateway to the west and central regions, Tampa has an international airport said to be one of the most efficient in the country. Its name was on a list of Indian towns recorded by Fontenado in 1580 and on de Laet's map of 1625. However, when de Soto landed here in 1539 to take possession of what was then an Indian village, the place was known as Espiritu Santo Bay. The first American settlement was established in 1823 when a log fort, Fort Brooke, was built. When troops left to join the Confederate forces in 1861, the town was left defenseless and the population dwindled.

In the 1880s new communications brought the return of people and power. Spanish and Cuban immigrants moved

In Busch Gardens, Tampa

here to work at cigar making. This influx resulted in the growth of the Spanish quarter, Ybor City, situated to the east of today's business district, bordering the Ybor Estuary and McKay Bay. When phosphate fields were discovered, in the 1890s, Tampa's deep-water port proved of great benefit to the export of the product.

Henry Plant saw its potential as a winter tourist resort and, in order to compete with Flagler in the east, built the Tampa Bay Hotel in 1891. It became an instant success. Plant spent a good deal of money developing the Tampa area and building a major port to accommodate his steamships.

See **Ybor City**, Tampa's historic quarter still housing a Cuban community. With its wrought-iron balconies, plazas, arcades and sidewalk cafes, it is an interesting area to browse through, especially around Ybor Square. There are shops, Spanish restaurants, a cigar factory and a newly opened winery.

The most popular theme park is **Busch Gardens/The Dark Continent**, a 300-acre entertainment park with 3000 animals, seven African theme sections, thrill rides, live entertainment and animal shows. Close by, Adventure Island is a seven-acre water theme park with slides, flumes and wave pool. Also visit Aquamania where each of four slides are over 400 ft. long. For small children, Fairyland Park and Zoo in Lowry Park spreads over ten acres with lifesize fairytale figures.

You can drive or take a boat or helicopter to Bahia Beach Island Resort and Marina in Tampa Bay, offshore from Ruskin. This full-service resort features boating, fishing charters, tennis, mini golf, swimming and sunbathing. Accommodations include hotel rooms and apartments. Championship golf courses are close by and bike, boat and jet ski rentals are available on the 124-acre island. Accommodations in Tampa include a Hyatt Regency, Marriott, Holiday Inn and Hilton.

HMS Bounty, *St. Petersburg*

Jungle Gardens, Sarasota

Ybor City, Tampa

Greek community, Tarpon Springs

Tarpon Springs   E3

(pop. 7118) Founded in 1876, Tarpon Springs is part of the Pinellas Coast. It lies at the point where the Anclote River widens into bayous on its way to the Gulf. The first settlers thought that tarpon spawned in the spring's bayou – hence the name – but the fish found in the river and lagoons here are, for the most part, mullet. Saw manufacturer, Hamilton Disston from Philadelphia, bought land round the springs in the 1880s and persuaded others to join his settlement. He built a hotel to accommodate them and for a decade this was the sole fashionable resort on the Gulf Coast.

In 1905, with the improvement in deep-sea diving equipment, Greek sponge fishermen moved here from Key West. They abandoned the old method of hooking sponges from shallow water and took to using diving gear far out to sea. The place is still very Greek – and still full of sponges.

The life of the Greek community revolves round Dodecanese Boulevard and the Sponge Docks, and you'll find Greek restaurants and Greek gifts in the boutiques here. See also **St. Nicholas Greek Orthodox Cathedral**, a replica of St. Sophia's in Istanbul. It is an exceptional example of Neo-Byzantine architecture. The interior features sculpted marble and stained-glass windows. The church is the focal point of the Blessing of the Fleet during Epiphany in January.

See also **Spongeorama**, a complex with dioramas, film and a spongers' village depicting the history of the sponge industry. 19th-century American landscape painter, George Inness, built a house and studio on a slope overlooking Spring Bayou. His son also worked here and the largest single collection of George junior's paintings (mostly religious) are displayed in the Universalist Church of Tarpon Springs. A short drive along the causeway takes you to Fred Howard Park and Sunset Beach, Tarpon Springs' Gulf beach and park with picnic facilities and a children's playground.

Tarpon Springs is noted for its many festivals and colorful atmosphere. Specialized resort accommodations within the vicinity include Saddlebrook Golf & Tennis Resort in Wesley Chapel and Innisbrook Golf Resort in Tarpon Springs. Riding enthusiasts can saddle up for trail riding at Melody Dude Ranch.

Treasure Island   G3

(pop. 6120) A Pinellas resort with almost four miles of white sand beaches that make it famous. Treasure Island has some of the widest stretches of sand to be found along the Suncoast. You can walk the island's length and there are lifeguards and cabanas along the way.

Watersports are top priority. Sailboats, paddleboats and windsurfing boards can be rented at the southern end of the island and instruction is available. At the northern end, Johns Pass is *the* Pinellas fishing center but you can also fish from any beach, bridge, pier or seawall or, of course, from a charter boat. Treasure Island has its own par three golf course and there are many more located within an easy drive. The Paradise Island tennis complex offers 21 courts which are open to the public.

THE NORTHWEST

The Florida Panhandle. That's the name given to this historic and beautiful region because of its shape. A narrow strip of land with dazzling white sands, salt marshes, rolling hills and pine forests, it stretches from Pensacola to the Suwannee River.

In many ways the northwest is more rural and easygoing than much of the rest of the state. It has an Old South mentality and charm enhanced by old plantation houses, magnolias and moss-laden oaks. History before the Civil War reveals itself in place names like Tallahassee, Okaloosa and Apalachicola from Indian cultures. Early Spanish settlements were founded here – such as Santa Rosa and San Marcos – before the British and Americans made their imprint.

The northwest encompasses the state's largest national forest, Apalachicola, plus 25 state parks. Outdoor opportunities are legion. There are more canoe trails (including the longest of all) than in any other region, over 100 campgrounds and many excellent facilities for swimming, boating and picnicking.

From its 200-mile coastline to its crystal-clear springs and scattered lakes and rivers, there are rich rewards for the fisherman. It is one of the world's best billfishing grounds. Charter boats leave from Pensacola, Fort Walton Beach, Destin, Panama City and Apalachicola in search of tuna, sailfish and marlin on half-, full-day or week-long trips. Bass is the prize in inland lakes such as Jackson, Talquin, Miccosukee, the Dead Lakes and Lake Seminole. Inshore grass flats along the coast yield redfish, speckled trout and the like.

Unsullied beaches, 100 miles of sugar white sands where one can hide away, give great appeal to the northwest. And there are islands to escape to such as Shell Island near Panama City Beach. Beaches and islands form a contrast to the industry of modern northwest Florida. Pensacola, Pensacola Beach and other adjacent communities support a major chemical industry, an oil and natural gas field and a large naval base.

Boat trips, camp/canoe trips, spelunking tours are all possible in the northwest. But for those who prefer to stay put, resort properties are on the increase in the oceanfront communities of Destin, Fort Walton Beach and Panama City, catering to the increasing numbers of people who have discovered that the northwest is somewhere special. (The state's best-kept secret is out.)

You'll find golf and tennis facilities all along the coast and inland. There are two PGA tournament venues – Pensacola's Perdido Bay Country Club and Tallahassee's Lillearn Golf & Country Club. Bluewater Bay Resort, off the Intracoastal Waterway, has added an 18-hole championship golf course and offers villas and townhouses for rent on a daily or package basis. Seascape Resort, in Destin, features villas and two-bedroom townhouses within walking distance of their golf course, across from the Gulf of Mexico. Bay Point Resort in Panama City offers villas for rent and has its own nine-hole golf course. A get-away-from-it-all place, the Pelican Club on Dog Island, is situated on a 1600-acre barrier island off the coast of Carrabelle. It has fully-furnished, well-equipped, gulf-side apartments.

For amusements, Panama City Beach is probably best. Its Miracle Strip provides a concert facility right next to the amusement park. The Flamingo Hotel has a dome-covered garden with pathways, benches and tables and tropical plants, while Alvin's Magic Mountain Mall has added a new look to the Gulf Coast city by incorporating shops, games rooms, restaurants and a radio station booth into what was an existing 'mountain' attraction on US 98. Miracle Mile has a new water-racing slide and Panama City's International Diving Museum at the downtown marina will prove interesting to those with a penchant for the sport.

Grand lady of the northwest is the state capital, Tallahassee, where the governor's mansion can be toured. Fashioned after Andrew Jackson's Tennessee home, the Hermitage, this mansion is furnished with many British antiques.

Apalachicola   F11
(pop. 3102) A town at the mouth of the

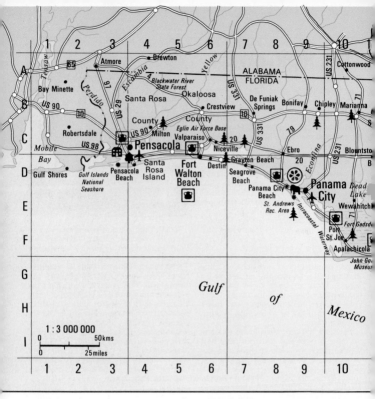

Apalachicola River, its name is taken from the Indian for 'people on the other side'. It produces 90 percent of Florida's oysters from some 10,000 acres of carefully tended oyster beds. Oyster shells are dropped on the beds to give young oysters a form of anchorage and to protect them from arch enemies such as the star fish. The beds are periodically raked with cotton mops attached to lengths of chain.

The site was known as early as 1528 when Narvaez camped on the shores of Apalachicola Bay though the town as such wasn't founded until 1821. It was incorporated as West Point in 1827, acquiring its present name in 1831.

Major point of interest is **Fort Gadsden Historic Site,** a 76-acre park on the site of a British fort destroyed in 1816 by American forces and later rebuilt by Lieutenant James Gadsden. You can picnic, fish, boat or find a nature trail here. Also look in at the **John Gorrie Museum** where exhibits honor the man who invented the ice-making machine. Dr John Gorrie, a resident of Apalachicola, invented his ice maker in 1845 and used it to cool

the rooms of patients sick with fever. His device was patented in 1851 but he was unable to raise the money to develop it commercially. He died in 1855, without gaining recognition for his work, and was buried in Magnolia Cemetery.

For pure recreation, St. George Island State Park has an excellent campsite and plenty of sport facilities.

Cedar Key I18

(pop. 714) A fishing village cum artists' colony on a white sand island three miles offshore in the Gulf of Mexico. At one time it was a busy port and railroad terminal. Hotels were built to accommodate passengers who had to transfer here to reach destinations in southern Florida. The surrounding islands were inhabited by pre-Columbian Timucuan Indians as you'll see from the number of burial mounds. Cedar Key (which tends to get crowded on weekends but is relatively quiet during weekdays) has hotels and an interesting museum set in 18 acres with dioramas depicting local history, and shell collections.

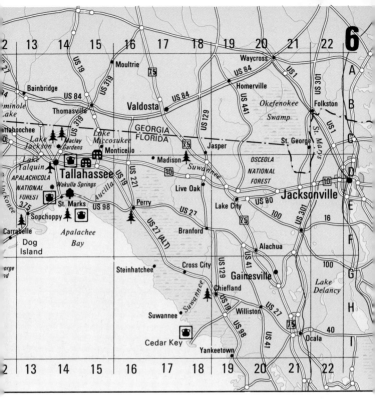

Destin   D6

(pop. 3600) Named for a sea captain, Destin used to be a small fishing village. These days it is tagged as 'Billfishing Capital of the Gulf' and many a charter boat departs from here. There are restored Indian burial grounds in the area and accommodations include Seascape Resort which has its own golf course, and a Holiday Inn.

Fort Walton Beach   D6

(pop. 22,200) *The* playground of the northwest and a lively beach center. It was built on the site of a fort of the same name which stood here at the time of the Seminole Wars. Today it is a fishing and yachting mecca with the added spark of having Eglin Air Force Base and Hurlburt Field (a military reservation) in its vicinity. The public fishing and observation pier stretches into the Gulf of Mexico for more than 1000 ft. Fishing opportunities range from trolling to surf or freshwater. Yachts participating in summer regattas make Fort Walton Beach their base.

The **Gulfarium and Shell Museum**

is an interesting marine attraction with giant sea turtles and porpoises among other creatures. By way of contrast, the **Indian Mound Museum** is a prehistoric Indian temple mound.

Fort Walton Beach has plenty of golf courses, tennis courts and clubs, marinas and diving centers. There are daytime or dinner/dance cruises along the Choctawhatchee River and train tours include Okaloosa Island and downtown. Among the plentiful accommodations are the Islander Beach Resort (on Okaloosa Island) and Bluewater Bay vacation community northeast of town.

Monticello   C15

(pop. 2473) Named for Thomas Jefferson's home near Charlottesville, Virginia, this is an agricultural district specializing in watermelons, pecans and satsuma oranges. The town was founded in the early 1800s by planters from Georgia and Carolina who worked the land around a block house that stood on the site of today's court house.

There are some beautiful antebellum

Suwannee River

Cedar Key

Indian Temple Mound Museum, Fort Walton

homes and plantations to be seen – one of the most famous is **Bellamy** on State 133. John Bellamy was one of three planters from South Carolina who settled in Florida and laid out and named Jacksonville (for General Andrew Jackson) in 1822. He became one of the wealthiest men in the States. The old family cemetery on the plantation grounds contains the graves of four generations of Bellamys.

Panama City Beach   E8

(pop. 1370) A favorite, vibrant beach resort with plenty of amusements. Best known is Miracle Strip Amusement Park which opens additional rides and attractions every year, including a new water-racing slide, and a zoo. Gulf World Aquarium gives daily shows and has several underwater exhibits. Snake-A-Torium is the largest reptile park in northwest Florida. A good place for viewing Panama City Beach is from the observation tower, 203 ft high, at Miracle Strip.

Watersports are number one here and boat cruises to the Gulf islands leave from St. Andrews State Recreation Area and Treasure Island Marina. At the downtown marina, an international Diving Museum explains the history of diving in the area.

At **St. Andrews Recreation Area** you'll find wide beaches and dunes, a restored 'cracker' (pioneer) turpentine still, nature trails and plenty of sport facilities. There's a choice of campsites in Panama City, including Seagrove Beach to the west which has beach access and its own pool. Other accommodations include Bay Point Resort and the Miracle Mile Resort's four hotels, plus the Flamingo Hotel whose 'Flamingo Dome by the Sea' is a dome-covered tropical garden with pathways, tables and benches. It has several rooms with their own kitchenettes.

Panama City Beach offers concerts in a facility next to Miracle Strip Amusement Park and has carved a shopping mall out of its 'mountain' attraction, Alvin's Magic Mountain Mall, which includes games rooms, restaurants and a radio station booth. A wide choice of restaurants and entertainment and festivities throughout the year keep Panama City Beach on the go. The Seafood Festival in October is one to make a note of.

Pensacola   C4

(pop. 66,500) Under the rule of five different flags since 1559, Pensacola, 'The City of Five Flags', is one of Florida's most historic cities. An industrial capital with a naval station, it is also an expanding tourist resort. On the north shore of Pensacola Bay, the city's deep-water port

is the largest, natural landlocked harbor in the US. To the east is Bayou Texar and to the west Bayou Chico – wide arms of the bay reaching inland on each side of the Pensacola peninsula. Ship channels ribbon past Fort San Carlos and Fort Barrancas and the US Naval Air Station, entering the Gulf of Mexico between a barren sand spit and Santa Rosa Island.

In all probability Panfilo de Narvaez and his men passed close by Pensacola in 1528, but recorded history begins with Captain Maldonado, commander of the fleet that bore de Soto to Florida. He named this place Puerta d'Anchusi, perhaps because the Indian name for the bay was Ochus. A subsequent expedition, under Don Tristan de Luna, renamed the place Santa Maria. The present name is thought to be derived from the Indian words *panshi*, meaning hair, and *okla*, meaning people – a nickname for the locals who wore their hair long. Some historians, though, claim that the name was taken straight from the Spanish seaport, Peñiscola.

At the outbreak of the American Revolution, Pensacola became a Tory base. This resulted in the Scottish businessman, William Panton, establishing his trading firm here and becoming America's first millionaire. Pensacola prospered from 1772. It was chartered as a city in 1822 and, in 1825, because of its strategic position and first-class harbor, the US set up a naval yard here.

At the start of the Civil War Pensacola was the state's largest city. But the Confederates were ordered to abandon the city and the years following the war left the place drowsy and in disrepair. It revived in the 1870s with the development of the waterfront and, by the turn of the century, it was the state's second largest city. In 1914 the government made it their first training base for naval aviators.

Today, history is the great attraction, especially in the **North Hill** preservation district, where homes built during the timber boom have been restored. A special rubber-tired tour train takes visitors through the district in open-air comfort, though air-conditioned coach tours are also available. The other historic district is **Seville Square**, where 18th- and 19th-century buildings have been renovated and interspersed with specialty shops and restaurants.

Two museums of note: **T.T. Wentworth Jr. Museum**, with 35,000 items of local historic interest, was the region's first proper museum. Aviation relics and models are on display at the **US Naval Aviation Museum**, and free guided bus tours take you past strategic military

Tallahassee: Governor's Mansion

State Capitol

points where historic battles took place.

Pensacola has beaches and boat excursions round the bay. A two-mile beachfront at Perdido Key State Preserve is open for day use. Santa Rosa Island is another option for a day's beachcombing. Miles of white sand, fishing, diving and all the other watersports are available at Pensacola Beach itself.

A striking view of the Gulf and Santa Rosa Island is to be had from an observation tower in Big Lagoon State Recreation Area (near Pensacola). The park has nature trails, boardwalks campsites and an outdoor amphitheater.

Accommodations include the Holiday Inn at Pensacola Beach which gives guests golfing privileges at nearby Santa Rosa Shores Country Club.

Tallahassee   D14

(pop. 87,400) The state capital city is situated about 30 miles north of the Gulf of Mexico, midway between Pensacola and Jacksonville. Tallahassee is an Indian word for 'old town', the name of the Apalachee Indian capital which was a flourishing settlement when de Soto and his men reached here in 1539. After the Spanish explorer left, a few missionaries and soldiers moved in and the rich farming land soon became a food source for St. Augustine and Fort St. Lewis, built in 1640 to serve as headquarters for seven missionary settlements.

Tallahassee was incorporated as a city in 1825. Streets were named for political celebrities, Adams, Monroe, Jefferson, as were squares, for Nathanael Greene and Andrew Jackson. With an eye to growing cotton, several leading families from other southern states moved here, turning the city into a social center where many galas and parties were hosted. It was the only southern capital east of the Mississippi which remained uncaptured during the Civil War.

Today, Tallahassee is responsible for state government and is a wholesaling, manufacturing and distribution center for

north Florida and south Georgia. The **State Capitol** is a sightseeing must. Built on a block-square terraced knoll overlooking the business district, the Capitol stands on South Monroe Street. When this site was chosen as the seat of government, no town existed and the legislative council met for the first time, in 1824, in a crude log cabin. The building was eventually completed in 1845, when Florida was admitted to statehood, and remained unchanged until 1902 when further additions were made.

One of the oldest houses is **The Columns** at the corner of North Adam Street and West Park Avenue. Built of red brick, in 1835, with a pitch roof and columned entrance, it has wide, vine-covered chimneys rising from the gable end. They say a nickel is embedded in every brick, but that has still to be proved! A mahogany staircase leads from the rear hall to the second floor, and the guide will tell you that one of the rich owners had this built through his bedroom to prevent his pretty daughter from leaving the house without his knowledge.

The state museum of historic items is in the R.A. Gray Building. Youngsters will appreciate the Tallahassee Junior Museum which has a pioneer farm, wildlife and a nature trail. The **Governor's Mansion** is open for free public tours on certain days of the week. It was fashioned after Andrew Jackson's Tennessee home, The Hermitage, and is furnished with 18th- and 19th-century antiques.

See Lake Jackson Mounds Archeological Site where de Soto spent the winter of 1539. **Maclay State Gardens** shows off masses of camellias, gardenias and azaleas, has a recreation area and guided tours of Maclay House. Just south of Tallahassee is **Wakulla Springs** where 600,000 gallons per minute flow from underground caverns to form the Wakulla River; it features glass-bottom boat rides, a recreation area and a museum.

Tallahassee accommodations include a Rodeway Inn, Holiday Inn and Sheraton.

INDEX

All main entries are printed in heavy type. Map references are also printed in heavy type.
The map page number precedes the grid reference.